Bitzaro to Buckingham

John Flanner

Published by John Flanner 2015

Printed by Biddles 2015

Biddles
Castle House,
East Winch Rd,
Blackborough End,
King's Lynn,
Norfolk
PE32 1SFX

A catalogue record for this book is available from the British Library.

ISBN 978-0-9934175-2-8

Typeset in Calibri 12pt by Rachel Edwards Writes.

Cover design by Studio D Creative.

Cover: Photograph of Buckingham Palace by David Iliff.
Licence CC-BY-SA 3.0

Printed in Great Britain.

Contents

Foreword

It never ceases to amaze me what mankind can endure and overcome with perseverance, positivity and prayer. Having always considered myself to be a 'glass half full' kind of girl, I try to see the good in every person and everything, despite the circumstances I find myself in. However had I have been faced with the trials and tribulations that have presented themselves before the Flanners' I can't help but wonder if my smile would have faltered on more than one occasion. Yet this extraordinary couple have defied their challenges and turned them into God-breathed opportunities to share their love for others, and in doing so sharing the very gospel that is core to their faith. Their unswerving loyalty to God and their complete trust in Him inspires me greatly, and not least because as John's story unfolds so too do the gifts that have been placed within him.

John Flanner is an exceptionally gifted writer and speaker. He writes in much the same way as he speaks, with infectious enthusiasm and genuine care for the audience as he draws you in to the tales of his life, detailing twists and turns that may reflect something of your own journey. Editing John's books has been an honour and privilege for me and as I read the text over and over, I often found myself moved to tears at the drama within the pages or bursting into spontaneous laughter at John's incredible sense of humour. Whether you are a businessman or a stay at home mom, I can guarantee that you will find encouragement and wisdom within these pages and this true story of a faithful husband and wife will forever change your outlook on life for the better.

Enjoy!

Rachel Edwards, Writer and Editor at Rachel Edwards Writes

Endorsement

I have known John for over forty years, his incredible personality has undoubtedly attracted many people to attend his seminars over the years.

John faced the heart breaking news of pending blindness at a time in life when most are just planning their future - his personal faith and stoic determination to overcome difficulties has left a legacy for others to learn from.

I personally experience a depth of insight from John that must be of value to a community who often ignore the values of life in the quest for survival. John speaks with conviction yet, relationally, he speaks as if he has known his listeners as personal friends.

I would highly recommend John to any business or community that wants to be inspired to reach their destiny.

Rt Revd Dr David E Carr OSL

Bishop, Order & Community of St Leonard
David E Carr OSL
Renewal Christian Centre
Free Methodist Church.

Chapter 1 - A Holiday to remember

I awoke at about 6am to the terrifying noise of what sounded like my dear wife choking to death. I shouted at her to wake up and on getting no response, jumped out of bed and ran round to the other side. I then began to shake her and yelled "Sylvia wake up, if you can hear me squeeze my hand".

There was no response and the sound coming from her, similar to that of someone gargling, was getting louder by the second. Being totally blind myself I had no idea whatsoever what her facial expressions looked like. Thinking that she may be having a fit, I tried in vain to roll Sylvia on to her side and into the recovery position. Having only partially succeeded I ran back around the bed to ring hotel reception to request they get a Doctor. Before I had made the call however, Sylvia sat up and quite calmly asked "What were you doing and why was there panic in your eyes?"

I said, "You are so right there was panic in my eyes, I thought you were choking to death or having a fit or something".

"No" said Sylvia, "I just had some acid reflux in my throat and I was simply trying to clear it".

I did not know whether to believe that or not, but Sylvia did sound better and quite with it, so I thought to myself maybe I did panic unnecessarily after all. I got back into bed and lay there holding her tightly as she went back into a peaceful sleep until it was time to arise for breakfast.

We were staying at the Bitzaro Palace Hotel on the Greek island of Zante. This was our fourth time holidaying at the same hotel and we continued going back there simply because it was a lovely quiet resort and the staff were so incredibly friendly. It was so reassuring each time we returned to be greeted as long lost family with lots of hugs and kisses from so many members of staff.

This one week holiday coincided with the announcement back in the UK that I had been awarded an MBE in the Queen's Birthday Honours List for my work within HMRC, actively promoting Diversity and Equality as well as for inspiring people across the Civil Service with my motivational talks. Now this joyous occasion was about to turn into one of the biggest nightmares of my life.

Having enjoyed our typical holiday breakfast of fruit with yoghurt, bacon, eggs and tomatoes followed by tea and toast, we sat in the delightful gardens of the hotel for a while, sipping a fruit juice and sheltering from the already hot morning sunshine. Hotter than usual we were told for early June. We then took a short walk to get a newspaper, Daily Mirror these days, because we loved solving the three crosswords together.

After a gentle stroll back, Sylvia's talking seemed a little laboured, so we went back to our room and sat on our balcony for a short time. Sylvia then said, "Do you mind if I go in for a lie down?"

Of course I did not mind in the slightest because I would just sit out on the balcony enjoying the lovely warm breeze (no sun on that side until the afternoon), and have a quiet little pray for family and other folk back home. The trouble was that Sylvia slept for a long time. I kept going back inside to check she was still breathing however she seemed very peaceful and figuring she probably had a very disturbed night, I decided to let her sleep on.

Sylvia awoke at about 3.15pm and said "Let's go for lunch".

"Too late", I said, "we have missed it".

On realising the time Sylvia apologised profusely, but I said not to worry because, as we were all inclusive, we could go to the pool side bar and get a sandwich or a burger.

We went to eat, but all the time Sylvia was apologising for losing track of time. I said I would have a cheeseburger and Sylvia said she would have the same however she only had a couple of bites out of hers and then gave it to me to finish. They were very big burgers and even with my healthy appetite, I found it hard to eat both of them. We then drank our diet cokes and headed out for a little walk before returning to our room to commence our attempts on the crosswords. The rest of the day passed by fairly uneventfully and I had no idea of the horrors that lay just ahead of us.

The next morning on our way to the dining room for breakfast, Sylvia, walking slightly slower than usual said hesitantly, "I am sorry, but I cannot remember the way".

She wandered around the swimming pool before actually locating the dining room and guiding me in to a table for two. We proceeded through breakfast with Sylvia telling me she did not feel quite right and that instead of sitting out in the gardens as usual, she would prefer to go back to our room.

On getting back she decided to lie down and rest her head so I took up my usual place on the balcony to commence my earlier than usual prayer time. I then went back into the room to check on Sylvia and I noticed that she was breathing a little noisily and so I stayed with her for a while. The gurgling, gargling sound that I had heard the day before seemed to be returning and so I tried to wake Sylvia up by calling her and shaking her. Having no success I decided to waste no time and rang for a Doctor.

Within twenty minutes or so, the Doctor was in our apartment desperately trying to rouse Sylvia from her deep sleep. He introduced himself to me as Christos and even the sound of his name brought comfort and reassurance. He began to run the usual tests; blood pressure, temperature, ECG and so on. After a short while he discovered that the oxygen levels in Sylvia's blood were low and he asked if she suffered from asthma. Sylvia did manage to mutter some unintelligible words and I confirmed that every morning for around about twenty years she had endured a long bout of coughing on waking, which Doctors had described as a rare form of asthma. He asked if she took an inhaler, but I informed him that although she had originally been prescribed one, she did not get on too well with it, so she tried to manage without.

Dr. Christos then decided to give Sylvia an inhaler from his bag, showed her how to use it and instructed her to take two puffs into her mouth and inhale deeply. After a bit of a struggle, as she was still very sleepy, Sylvia managed to do this.

Christos did say that if Sylvia was a Greek citizen she would be admitted to hospital so that they could try and ascertain the root cause of her condition, but he fully appreciated we would want to get our flight home to Birmingham.

After about ten or fifteen minutes, Christos took the readings again and confirmed that Sylvia's oxygen level had gone up considerably. He decided that Sylvia should keep the inhaler and take two puffs before she went to bed that night and two more the next morning. He would then return and check her out again. I have to say, he was very warm, reassuring and I sensed more than just a little concerned.

The rest of the day passed by fairly uneventfully and though I was concerned about Sylvia's extreme lethargy, I put it down to the low oxygen levels the Doctor had talked about and reasoned that after a few more puffs of the inhaler things would improve. How wrong I was for I was about to encounter one of the most terrifying days of my life – certainly in the top three anyway!

Everything started off great on that Thursday morning, the day before we should have been flying home. Sylvia dutifully used the inhaler before going to bed on the Wednesday night and to my knowledge she had one of the soundest night's sleep she had enjoyed in a long time. Even better she went to the bathroom and did not cough for the first time in many years. "Well, what a miracle inhaler" I thought to myself, "all those years of needless coughing". Sylvia took a shower, then made drinks and we sat on the balcony enjoying the pleasant summer breeze before going down for breakfast. On the way (only a short distance) Sylvia again stopped and said "I don't know where I am".

I asked a passing holidaymaker to point us in the right direction for the dining room as my wife was feeling a little unwell and soon we were inside. Sylvia again stood rigid in the middle of the floor and anxiously said "I cannot remember our table number".

Trying to sound calm, I said, "There are no table numbers my love, we can sit anywhere".

I will never forget her reply because it was so clear, matter of fact and authoritative, "Oh I don't think so".

With that one of the very attentive waitresses sat us down at the table we were standing by and said "Sit here and I will get your fruit juice and yoghurt".

While the waitress was away, Sylvia said "I want to go back to our room, I am so frightened".

The waitress returned with our orange juice and our favourite starter and I asked if someone could shortly walk us back to our room because I wanted to call the Doctor to see Sylvia. The waitress gently touched my shoulder and said "Don't worry John, I have already called for him". Another staff member then guided us back to our apartment where Sylvia immediately lay down. Within a minute or so I spoke to her asking how she was feeling but I got no response so I began the now familiar shouting and shaking routine to no avail. Trembling, I dialled nine on the bedside phone to ask reception to help me as my wife had gone into a deep sleep. Takis, the Greek guy on duty that day, told me the Doctor was in the hotel and would be with me shortly. Almost immediately there was a knock on the door and I was so relieved to discover that it was Christos again.

He brushed passed me to get to Sylvia, who by this time had started to make those horrible gargling sounds again. I was told there was no option than to get Sylvia to hospital and in no time at all the ambulance arrived.

They took Sylvia away and I was told I was not allowed to go in the ambulance, but would travel by taxi accompanied by my good friend Takis from reception. Someone, maybe one of the ambulance men, or even Christos had passed on a message via Takis to alert me to the fact that Sylvia was very seriously ill and may not survive the day. They were numbing words, but they did not come as a surprise because twice in the previous couple of days I thought I was losing her.

It was surreal talking with Takis in the taxi about the World Cup in Brazil and how well Greece were doing compared to England, while my wife's life hung in the balance.

We soon arrived at the hospital and I was greeted by two very welcome English voices. Helen was a representative working for the British Consul in Zante and Elaine was an Administrator working for Thomson the travel company we had gone on holiday with. Both of these ladies were supportive and reassuring during those couple of hours while we waited for news of my beloved wife of 44 years.

At long last news came through that Sylvia was back and had been admitted to Ward 10 on the pathological wing of the hospital. Helen escorted me to the bedside and I was surprised and delighted to find Sylvia sitting up in bed to greet me. She sounded tired and frail, but very much alive and it was all I could do to hold my tears in as my body shook with absolute relief and emotion.

I had managed during the course of the morning to ring my children and Elizabeth, a close family friend from church. Our son, Ian, said he would make arrangements to fly out that night to be with me and what an incredible help he would prove to be over the next couple of weeks.

There were very few medical people at the hospital who could speak English so I was very grateful for Helen and Elaine who assisted me with translation. Via Helen, I discovered that Sylvia had almost certainly suffered a major stroke, followed by a fit and that the following 48 hours or so were crucial to her recovery.

Meanwhile Elaine informed me that there were no nurses on duty in that hospital, if I wanted nursing cover for Sylvia then I would have to pay private. It was customary for families to look after their own loved ones 24/7 and only in an emergency press the buzzer for a Doctor. I said that I did want the nursing cover so Elaine arranged for the first two days to be covered by three nurses working eight hour shifts. Holiday insurance would normally cover this, but I was advised not to worry myself over that, just wait for my son to arrive and then work it all out between us.

I left the hospital at about 10pm that night with Sylvia wired up to a variety of tubes and with oxygen going up her nose. She seemed as though she was in a most contented and peaceful sleep. I was escorted out of the hospital by two Greek ladies, who had been caring for a loved one on the same unit as Sylvia. They did not speak much English, but they did manage to say "Taxi" so I assumed they were going to help me get a taxi. When outside the hospital, they sat me down on a bench and began to talk noisily amongst themselves. Every now and again, the younger of the two women would come back, tap me on the shoulder and mutter "Taxi". Once I got up from my seat thinking she meant the taxi was there, but she forcibly made me sit down again. At that point I did start to feel a bit confused and dare I say, a little frightened.

All went quiet and it felt like the two ladies had disappeared, I could not hear them anywhere. I felt very alone and vulnerable. I recall uttering a desperate prayer "Oh God please deliver me from this Hell". Time moved on and I must have sat there for half an hour with apparently nothing happening. It was a warm, balmy evening and pretty dark by this time. I started to feel very alone and quite panicky, thinking here I am in a strange country, no one appears to speak English and to my side was a hospital in which to all intends and purposes my wife was lying close to death.

At long last I heard some voices; a man and a lady chatting away. As they passed by I arose from my seat and asked how I could get a taxi. They were both Greek people I think, but mercifully the man could understand and speak English, so I explained about my need to get a taxi. He kindly rang from his mobile and within a few minutes this part of my developing nightmare was at an end. The taxi ride back to Bitzaro Palace was quiet from a conversation point of view as the driver was listening to a commentary on one of the World Cup games. I am a keen football fan, but the World Cup in Brazil was far from my thoughts.

On arriving back to the hotel room I soon fell into an exhausted sleep for about four hours and then waited eagerly for my son to arrive at about 5am. I drifted in and out of sleep but was very alert when the knock on the door came and as Ian entered we locked in a tight embrace of love and tears. I gave Ian the low down on the current situation with Sylvia while he made a much needed cup of coffee, and as he did not feel like sleeping, we decided to set off on an early morning walk to the local beach just 15 minutes away. This small, idyllic cove was where Sylvia and I used to sit and eat an ice cream and part of the pretty little beach was cordoned off as the turtles like to lay their eggs there. Ian took photos of the beach and the kiosk (closed at that time of the morning) where Sylvia would get our ice creams from. He thought it would be nice to show her when she had recovered sufficiently to appreciate them.

As we travelled to the hospital by taxi there was a mixture of trepidation and excitement in our hearts. I think we were nervous about the state we might find Sylvia in and also excited by the fact she was going to see her son. We made our way quickly to the ward and despite the fact that Sylvia was talking to two other people, I heard her say very animatedly "My gosh, it's Ian".

Sylvia had been talking to Cliff and Maggie, a couple from Sutton Coldfield Baptist Church in the West Midlands who had moved out there six months before. They had received an email telling them about our plight and had decided to visit. Sylvia was reminiscing with them about people we mutually knew from that church and others in the area some 30 years or so before. It was a joy and not a little surprise to see her awake and so lively, although little did we know that we would not see her this bright again for the entire time we were in Zante.

Later that afternoon Sylvia fell into a deep sleep, developed a mystery virus and with it the ability, or perhaps the desire, to eat, drink or converse and her energy levels became almost non-existent. When the time came for us to leave to go back to our hotel we contented ourselves that sleeping was the best form of healing and that tomorrow would be different. How wrong we were!

On this day we had become aware that this small Greek hospital was very different to the ones back in the UK. Apart from having no nurses, except from the ones we had booked that is, the relatives stayed around all day long and for much of the night, often working in shift patterns and would care for their relatives so lovingly. The culture differences were stark, especially the usual practice of stripping a relative naked in front of everyone in order to wash them down. The Greek people also chat very noisily across the ward. There was a very communal, family feel to the whole thing, but it was a bit daunting if you were the one sick in bed and you did not speak their language and I know Sylvia found it to be extremely intimidating.

It was on this day that Ian's iPhone began to work overtime and did so for the entire length of our stay. He was constantly updating people back home via phone, texting, emails and Facebook. Soon news of Sylvia's illness had spread to several nations around the world and it was not long before the most amazing messages of support starting coming back. Ian also began the conversations with the insurance company as to exactly what we were covered for.

It was at this point we learned about the European Health Insurance Card (EHIC) that we should have carried with us. This card is available free and entitles individuals from European Union country to a level of free health care while visiting a fellow European Union country. Sylvia reads a daily newspaper, I am an avid radio listener and neither of us had ever registered the fact that we needed one of these precious free cards for such an emergency as this. Ian, who had also had several European holidays had not heard about it either. Thanks to the British Embassy and insurance company working together with Ian we did manage to get one faxed across so saving us a lot of expense for Sylvia's hospital stay.

We also have to admit that we did not take out the most suitable insurance cover. As with a lot of people, we took out the basic insurance, not thinking for one minute that we would need to avail ourselves of the air ambulance service, but it soon became apparent that is what we would need to aid Sylvia's recovery.

Bitzaro Palace is a quiet hotel with the minimum of entertainment, unlike its sister hotel Bitzaro Grande, just around the corner. On a Sunday night, however, they do have a guitar-playing singer come in for a couple of hours. It was Ian's second night with me and after the disappointment of seeing Sylvia deteriorate into an almost total unconscious state we were more than a little down-hearted.

Once back at the hotel and having had a bite to eat we went into the bar to have a listen to the singer. Obviously our emotions were a bit raw, but it seemed like the words of every song were applicable. I remember singing my heart out to *'You are my sunshine, my only sunshine, please don't take my sunshine away'*. It was like a prayer. Other songs he sang that night included *'Cupid'*, *'Brown-Eyed Girl'* and *'I'm a Believer'* and all of those contained lyrics which touched us deeply at the time. After a few drinks Ian and I headed back to our room, but I recall lying on the bed and we both gave a rendition of *'You Are My Sunshine'* before going off to sleep, hoping that tomorrow would bring an improvement in Sylvia's condition.

Day after day Sylvia continued to sleep. She had developed a mystery virus, her temperature was high and she sweat profusely. Her hands and arms were like pin cushions where she had had so many needles pushed in in an attempt to get blood as Doctors tried to ascertain just what kind of a virus this was.

One particularly sweltering afternoon in Zante, Ian took a well-deserved break from his fanning duties and took a walk to the local shops in search of some refreshment. I stayed at the bedside of Sylvia, holding and stroking the hand of my barely conscious wife. In the time that elapsed before Ian returned with two melon-flavoured ice lollies, I mused on the irony of our situation. My thoughts went something like this...

We came out here on the high of knowing I had just been awarded an MBE and would be going to Buckingham Palace, but now I may even lose my dear wife and am being cared for by the staff of Bitzaro Palace. Good title for a book I thought, 'Bitzaro Palace to Buckingham Palace'.

That night when we returned to the hotel, I telephoned updates on Sylvia's condition to family and friends back home. This included Elizabeth Webb who, in the course of conversation, said that we needed to look forward with hope and that there would be a way through all this, adding that, 'Bitzaro Palace to Buckingham Palace' could be the title for my next book! I was almost dumbstruck as I recounted my experience in the afternoon when the exact same title had dropped in to my mind. Elizabeth described this as a 'faith moment' since, at the particular time, nothing seemed further from possibility. I later discovered that she had also sent this suggestion as a text message to Ian. What you are reading now is the result of those 'God-incidences' on that poignant day.

I must stress to you that this really was a most worrying time for Ian and me as we watched Sylvia struggling to stay awake. Ian and the nurse on duty would apply water to her lips, wipe her down with a flannel and fan her; there was no such thing as an electrical fan, just a paper one we went out and bought from a local shop. This was a dark and difficult time for us, but there were some brilliant shafts of light, which illustrated God's kindness to us. Whilst I have lots of questions about healing, I have no doubts whatsoever that God is faithful and kind, a loving Father indeed.

In my experience when God provides, He more often than not does so through people. In this case, the staff at Bitzaro Palace were truly amazing in their love and support. Not only did they provide Ian and me with a most generous packed lunch every day, but regularly staff from the hotel visited Sylvia. Some of the wonderful staff that showed us such kindness and compassion during that time included Stella the manager, Petra the senior receptionist, Marina the night receptionist, George the soup waiter and even the gardener who sent two separate bunches of gorgeous roses from his well-manicured gardens. Then, on the third day an English lady was admitted to the hospital and she was in the adjacent bed to Sylvia. Chrissy was 70 years of age and had married Ron only a short time before. Ron had been seriously ill so Chrissy thought she would be not only his wife, but carer too but now cruelly Chrissy had been struck down with cancer and was undergoing chemotherapy. She had been admitted to the Zante hospital, not far from their home, because she had suffered a serious asthma attack due to the extreme heat.

Chrissy was just the right person for Sylvia in that she spoke English and she was a great encourager. Ian and I were thrilled and contented to know that when we left the hospital at night, God had provided his own little angel to watch over Sylvia. I will never forget Chrissy as long as I live for the part she played in supporting Sylvia at a most vulnerable time.

After a week with no obvious signs of Sylvia improving; still in bed with a catheter, still not eating or drinking or speaking, it was decided that our oldest daughter Beverley would fly out to offer support to Ian and I as well as be there for her Mum. Our other daughters, twins Sara and Allison, were also back home feeling helpless but due to family commitments and no up to date passports it was not possible for them to fly over at that stage.

It was wonderful to see Beverley and give her a great big hug. Due to her midday arrival time, she was able to take a taxi direct to the hospital where Ian met her and brought her up to Ward 3. While Ian had been waiting in the foyer for Beverley to arrive, Sylvia had been moved from Ward 10 to another ward where she would remain for the rest of her stay.

We had several meetings with Doctors, but it was often difficult to get the full picture of Sylvia's overall condition and of the ongoing treatment and prognosis due to the language barrier. I could not help but reflect on the seeming irony that back at the hotel everyone spoke English but at the hospital hardly anyone did. Eventually when we did find a Doctor who could communicate more efficiently with us we discovered they were struggling to identify the virus which had afflicted Sylvia and sent her temperature soaring. The general consensus was that it would be much better if we could fly back to the UK and get her treated in a hospital where they had much more in the way of diagnostic equipment and appropriate treatment. We were told she could be in this sleepy state for weeks or months before they managed to get to the bottom of the problem.

That night I chatted on the phone with our good family friend Elizabeth Webb back in Solihull and I floated an idea by her. I felt a sense of urgency about getting Sylvia home, having been told that the longer we leave it the less chance she had of making a full recovery from the stroke. I wondered if a local newspaper would like to pick up on this story, i.e. a Solihull man goes on holiday to celebrate being awarded the MBE in the Queen's birthday honours only for this joyous occasion to turn into a nightmare. I thought if they ran the story their readers may wish to club together to raise the money to send for the UK Air Ambulance to come to our rescue. Elizabeth's daughter Rachel, who had just gained a qualification in Broadcast Journalism, apparently had a connection with the Birmingham Mail, so it was looking like a good avenue to go down.

At this time, it was via Facebook that we received some of our most encouraging and uplifting messages in our hour of need, with special mention going to Kate Hayes who rallied the troops by posting "Can someone start an appeal to get Sylvia home. They are well known in Solihull and from their previous church. She is our sister in Christ and we are family, there must be a way to raise £25,000 to get her home by air ambulance?" In the meantime though Ian and Beverley were saying to me that we should hold back a little to see what the insurance company would come up with.

This began a period of several days where Ian was in negotiations with Allianz Global UK with whom we had taken out our insurance, albeit not enough to cover the cost of an air ambulance. Though it had required some straight talking and hard bargaining, Ian managed to persuade Allianz Global to not just co-operate, but actually to go over and above what was required. They could have dug their heels in and refused to fly us home, but to their eternal credit they had compassion on our situation and began the procedure to get the air ambulance in place to fly us back to Birmingham.

While all of this was taking place, friends back home were saying in response to my newspaper request that it would be a travesty if they could not raise the money due to the fact that we were people who were active Christians and had been known in and around Solihull for many years. As a result, I understand that offers of help and pledges of money were offered over a three day period totalling around £25,000. What a truly wonderful expression of love for us that was, but thanks to Allianz Global UK and their willingness to overlook our deficient insurance cover, we did not have to call on our friends to personally fund our treatment and return journey.

On the back of our experience in Zante, Allianz Global UK later released a press release to highlight our plight and hopefully prevent anyone else being in our unfortunate situation. This press release can be seen in the appendices at the back.

While Sylvia lay critically ill in hospital, arrangements were being put in place behind the scenes for the insurance company's air ambulance to fly us back to the UK. In addition, the ongoing support we received from the senior management at Bitzaro Palace was truly outstanding. During our extra stay of twelve days we had to move hotels three times, but it was all arranged for us by Stella, the manager and Petra the head receptionist. We were also told that Ian, Beverley and I could come back and eat at Bitzaro Palace in the evenings for free. On the last day of our stay in Zante we needed 800 Euros to pay the nurses who had been looking after Sylvia and I could only obtain 300 Euros from the cash machine using my Barclays debit card. On hearing this, Stella gave us the 800 Euros and said we could pay it back any time.

When the day finally came to say goodbye there were lots of hugs and tears from so many members of staff, it felt like I was emigrating and saying a fond farewell to close family members. Unlike Sylvia and myself, for whom this was our fourth visit, Ian and Beverley had only been there a few days, yet they felt the warmth of this compassion too.

So eighteen days after the start of what was to be a celebratory holiday, Tuesday 1st July finally arrived and Sylvia was heading home. Not the way she intended of course, this was a very different departure, but one very big step forward on her road to what we hoped would be a full recovery.

We had been at the hospital for about an hour when we were told the ambulance had arrived to take Sylvia and me to the airport. Sylvia, though drowsy, was aware that she was going home courtesy of a medical ambulance and she was reassured to know I would be travelling with her.

The ambulance guys wheeled Sylvia on to the lift and down to the ground floor with Ian guiding me and Beverley alongside. When we arrived at the ambulance Ian and Beverley said their goodbyes to us, trying hard to hold back the tears as Sylvia was put into the small, hot ambulance and I was somehow squeezed in beside her. The 15 minute drive to Zakynthos Airport turned out to be the most uncomfortable of the whole journey. It was a very jerky ride and I felt sure Sylvia could feel every bump in the road as I heard her painful groans.

It was not long, however, before we were at the airport and we were being introduced to the medical team who would be looking after Sylvia. I did not catch the name of the Doctor but the two male nurses were introduced to me as Alex from Scotland and John from Italy, who, to my great relief, spoke the Queen's English. There was also a cabin crew member named Bridget, who was there to look after me. We also had two pilots which felt somewhat comforting!

Not being able to see, it is hard for me to explain the layout on the plane, but it felt quite small with me sat on the left hand side and Sylvia the other side of the aisle on a bed. In front of me was the Doctor, who was constantly it seemed monitoring Sylvia's blood pressure, temperature, sugar levels etc. At one point he told me he was giving her some glucose through the cannula as her sugar levels had dropped. From time to time he did turn around and tell me she was doing okay. The nurses would also pass by and check I was okay, as did Bridget who served me an excellent salami salad sandwich on Italian bread and a refreshing cup of fruit juice.

The journey itself including taking off and landing was overall pretty smooth. We did stop off at Antwerp in Belgium in order to pick up two more sick passengers and another Doctor, but then it seemed no time at all before we were landing in Birmingham and never did coming home feel so wonderful.

We were soon transferred to a waiting ambulance – it was great not to have to hang around at Passport Control or Baggage Reclaim! Even better was the news that we were being taken to Solihull Hospital and not the bigger Heartlands Hospital in Birmingham. This new venue would literally be within walking distance of where we live so just great for me as a hospital visitor.

Wonderfully, the Doctor assigned to us by the insurance company did not leave us until Sylvia was safely booked on to a ward. Once satisfied that she was comfortable, the Doctor then left to stay overnight in a Birmingham hotel where she was going to watch Belgium play in the World Cup that night.

I have already alluded to God's kindness in putting people in the right place at the right time. There was Helen from the British Consulate when I first arrived at the hospital in Zante, Cliff and Maggie formerly of Sutton Coldfield who visited Sylvia on a number of occasions during her hospital stay, there was Chrissie the English lady who encouraged and chivvied Sylvia along and now there was Kate.

More than 20 years earlier Kate had worked with Sylvia and our daughter Sara as a care assistant in Willow Grange Residential Home for the Elderly in Olton, Solihull. Now Sara was back working there and she bumped into Kate for the first time in many years during one of her shifts. It turned out that Kate, who had once lived with us for a while when she was in need, was now a Senior

Stroke Assessor for the Birmingham and Solihull areas. Some would say, these are nothing more than coincidences and maybe they are. On the other hand, many like me, have found the more you pray, the more 'coincidences' you seem to have.

Once Sylvia had gone through the admission procedures she was admitted to Ward 9 at Solihull Hospital, which is a specialist stroke unit that is sadly under threat of closure due to Government cuts in the NHS. We were saddened to learn during our time at the hospital that nearby Ward 10 and the invaluable Dementia Ward is also threatened with closure. Now it was time for Sylvia's recovery to really begin to kick in. With the increased medical expertise and dedicated around the clock nursing together with those familiar English voices, she was soon on an upward curve. Most noticeable to us as family was that Sylvia quickly became much more aware of what was going on and all of her normal bodily functions began to return. That was to me a great relief I have to say because there were times back in Greece, when I really doubted that would be the case.

Apart from landing back in the UK, one of my most cherished memories will always be that first night home after seeing Sylvia safely ensconced in her hospital bed. When I arrived back home, put my key in the door and sat down in my very own lounge and sat in my favourite armchair, I breathed a sigh of relief that I was home at last and it felt wonderful. Now the nightmare of the previous two weeks could begin to become a distant memory.

In all Sylvia spent ten days in Solihull Hospital and during that time made fantastic (some would say miraculous) progress. I think the key to her recovery was identifying and treating that mysterious virus which had afflicted her as once that was identified and being properly treated, the improvement was almost instant. Quickly, I am told, she began to look better and her speech was nice and clear. The catheter which she had for two weeks was removed and she was able to toilet herself immediately and without any real problems, and gradually her appetite began to return, though that is still needing to improve.

The physiotherapists and occupational therapist were a constant source of irritation to Sylvia as she always felt they were pushing her one step too far and too hard. They had her standing, walking, bending, catching and even exercising her throat muscles by singing. Most of the time she was not amused but deep down I think she knew it was for the best, however I think she just felt totally exhausted and wanted to sleep.

Popularity does come with a price of course and there is no doubt Sylvia is much loved judging by the many visitors that she received, which is not surprising really given the fact that she is a beloved mother, grandmother and friend. In addition she had more than 15 years' experience working as a carer in nursing homes and for Marie Curie Cancer care as well as long running links with several local churches. Though we were only supposed to have two at a bed at any one time there were several occasions when there were eight, nine or even ten visitors all at once. We were aware this was very exhausting for Sylvia, but it became logistically very difficult controlling the numbers though myself and our kids did our best to try and regulate visits, or limit people to 15 minutes at a time. As I said though, there is a price to be paid for being popular and in such instances people were only wanting to express their love. In many cases folk were offering much needed prayers of faith on Sylvia's part for which we were all very grateful.

The day of Sylvia's discharge came as almost a big surprise as her original illness. By this time I had returned to work at HM Revenue and Customs in Birmingham and just before leaving at 1pm to go and visit, I received a message from my son Ian to say that Sylvia could go home. Shocked, but excited, I got to the hospital as quickly as I could and together with Ian and Alison I waited eagerly for the discharge letter and accompanying medication. It felt like a long time hanging around and I know Sylvia was starting to feel a bit edgy too, but the time did come. Allison pushed Sylvia in a wheelchair while Ian went to get the car. When outside the hospital I heard Sylvia say "This is wonderful, I can't believe it". I think those words could have been echoed by anyone of us, but particularly by those of us who were with her in Zante, when everything seemed so bleak. Now back home and in familiar surroundings, the long road towards physical, mental and emotional wholeness was about to begin.

Our daughter Allison moved back from Falmouth to assist with Sylvia's day to day care. As a family we had moved to Cornwall twenty eight years ago so I could attend Bible College. After four years with me unable to find work, we moved back to Solihull, but Allison, who was then 17 years of age and undertaking a nursery nursing course at College, decided she wanted to stay there. Her decision to move back to the Midlands was therefore a giant step for her and one which we deeply appreciated. Thankfully she would also have support from our other three children Beverley, Sara and Ian.

I have already mentioned how great the staff at Bitzaro Palace were and even after we arrived home we continued to receive such kind emails from members of staff enquiring as to Sylvia's condition. I tell you if anyone is looking for a truly lovely, quiet holiday in a nice resort, at a genuinely family friendly hotel, I doubt you would find a hotel more loving and caring than Bitzaro Palace in Zante – oh yes the food is great too!

Now with memories of Bitzaro Palace behind us, we must start to focus on Buckingham Palace. I was told we would receive five weeks' notice of the date I was to go and receive my MBE from Her Majesty the Queen's official residence. Sylvia is a devout Royalist and so I prayed it would be as late in the year as possible so as to give her the maximum amount of time to recover her strength and accompany me on my journey down to London.

To explain in more detail what I have been awarded the MBE for, I must take you back 10 years.

Chapter 2 - Belief and breakthrough

I was working as an audio typist for the Inland Revenue, now Her Majesty's Revenue and Customs (HMRC), in Birmingham city centre. I trained as a typist shortly after going blind and apart from a couple of short spells doing other things, I had been a typist for many years and so at the age of 57 I was stuck in a very happy little rut. I had no idea that things were about to change so dramatically. As a regular speaker in local churches, one of my favourite messages had been "Big Doors Swing on Small Hinges" and little did I know a big door of opportunity was about to open for me. It all hinged on me agreeing to write an article for our office newsletters, as I had been asked to write about life in an ever-changing workplace from the viewpoint of a person with a disability.

When I came to write the article it flowed very freely from my fingertips to the keyboard and was done and dusted in about 20 minutes. I played the article back through my headphones using my screen-reader called JAWS (Job Access With Speech) and I must confess to being pretty pleased with what I heard. Within a few days the article was in print and being circulated around our building of about 1,000 Civil Servants. There were one or two polite comments from people on my team and others who passed by my desk, but it was a phone call that brought me the encouragement which was about to transform my life.

I picked up the phone to hear the voice of one of our Area Directors.

"Hi John, its John Dolan here and I just want to congratulate you on a wonderful article you have written. It is so informative and very humorous"."

My heart began to race and my chest began to swell with pride, but there was more to come as John continued....

"I have learned so much from this and I intend to pass it around my fellow Directors. Did anyone ever tell you, you have great communication skills?"

"No," I said "they never did."

"Well you have and judging by the way the Department is changing and developing, I think we may be able to make use of your talents in the days that lie ahead so very well done indeed."

I was still expressing my thanks as he put the phone down. Honestly the feel good factor and the warm glow lasted for days. Never in all my life had I received such glowing praise and affirmation... and there was more to come.

After three or four days John sent me an email in which he repeated all of the same wonderful things he had said on the phone. I played the email several times in fact because the words were doing me a power of good. In fact so thrilled was I by the email, I printed it off so I could take it home to show Sylvia my wife to remind her what a fantastic bloke she was married too. After all most of us in a relationship for more than five minutes do tend to take one another for granted don't we!

Well right at the end of this email the Area Director said that he had been thinking about me and my communication skills and wondering how he could develop me and give me the necessary tools to build my confidence. His suggestion was that I applied to go on a one year personal development programme called *Breakthrough* which entailed attending training one day a week for a year, to include a series of assignments and a project. As much as I appreciated all of the kind words John had said to me, the thought of going on a training programme for one day, let alone one year, scared me stiff. As I said before, I was in a happy little rut in a job I enjoyed and at the age of 57 was coasting my way towards retirement. I acknowledged John's email with grateful thanks, but made no mention of the *Breakthrough* programme, hoping he would just forget it.

How very wrong I was, as John was very shortly back on the phone asking what I was going to do about the *Breakthrough* training.

I responded sheepishly "Well I am 57 years of age and…."

Before I could finish with my excuses for not applying, John snapped back "Did I mention anything about age?"

"No." I said.

"And neither should you. All I am looking at is how we can develop you so that you can better utilise your talents later in your career".

After offering my apologies, I set to work with my manager in putting together my application and a week or two later I received the email to say I had been accepted and that the course would be held in Coventry.

This was clearly a watershed moment in my life. For many years I had practised being an encourager, because I knew how much encouragement meant to me. Encouragement permeated the whole of my life. As a keen football fan and a supporter of Aston Villa I fervently believed in getting behind the team and it puzzled me, how as a supporter, you could even consider booing your own team or ridiculing one of your own players who might be having a bad game. No one goes out to play badly, but sometimes you just have one of those days when nothing seems to go right and it is at these exact times that it would best boost the players if the supporters (I prefer that to fans, which I presume is short for fanatics!) actually chanted his name, got behind him and gave him some encouragement.

As a child I remember how devastating it was when I struggled with my maths homework, for my well-meaning Dad to say in frustration "You're stupid you are".

Going further back, when I was in infant school and we had school assemblies, I loved singing songs like *All Things Bright and Beautiful* and *If You Are Happy and You Know It*. In the early days I sang out with great gusto, until an older boy behind me, jabbed me firmly in the ribs and said "shut up you sound like a foghorn". I had never even heard of a foghorn at the time, but his words were suffice to shut me up for many years in fact. From then on I only ever mimed in school assemblies and at other events like weddings and baptisms. All of my family sang at home, but not me. I loved music and had hundreds of records that I played but I never sang along while others where there. I even wanted to sing in the bath, but did not for fear others might be listening.

I am different now, because as a Christian I have discovered that God loves it when we make a joyful noise. He does not require that we have a perfect, or even a tuneful voice. He just wants to hear a heart that is rejoicing in the precious gift of life. I love life so I sing on and even with all of my vocal deficiencies I know I can spread plenty of joy around.

I used to think it was just me who had been affected in this way, but even as I am writing this book, BBC Radio 2 have been doing a feature about *"The Rock Choir"* and one of the members joined because she had the same experience as me at school. She loved singing, but then a teacher told her to be quiet as she was singing badly. From then on until well into her adult life she only ever mimed because she was afraid to sing out. Now she is part of *"The Rock Choir"* and she enjoys belting out the songs for all she's worth as she makes up for lost time. The response to that interview was that hundreds of people wrote in to *Good Morning Sunday*, the programme running this feature, to say that they were similarly stifled as kids by being told to "shut up"...

Encouragement is powerful stuff, literally putting courage into people and helping set them free from negative and life-crushing words.

I really enjoyed *Breakthrough*, looking forward to every session. Sometimes we listened to a lecture and at other times we sat around a table in groups of about six, discussing topics and sharing experiences. Some of the themes covered were:

- The power of words
- What do you say about yourself
- Dreams and visions
- The power of forgiveness

- Developing goal setting skills
- The law of attraction.

The *Breakthrough* programme certainly achieved what it was meant to do in my case.

One of the most powerful sessions for me came when each of the delegates was given a set of blank postcards. There was a card for each of the delegates and we had to write on the card what positive characteristics struck you about each person. When we came back after lunch there was a pack of cards on each of our chairs and we were able to read all of the comments that the other people had said about us. Obviously I had to have one of the trainers read mine out to me and I was genuinely shocked, surprised and incredibly empowered by what people had said. Almost every card said I was inspirational and others said I had a great sense of humour, was a lot of fun, kind, caring, imaginative, encouraging and so on. Later one of the trainers pointed out that these comments were genuine; they were anonymous and there was no flattery and he encouraged us to be comfortable with our attributes and allow them to shape our lives. I think that this session was a real eye-opener (no pun intended) for me.

Next thing to face up to was the project. Oh yes the dreaded project! The brief was that the project we came up with needed to be something that would benefit the business, and I was completely stumped as to what I could possibly come up with that would benefit the HMRC. My old misgivings began to come back to haunt me as I thought to myself, "What can I do to benefit the business? I am just a typist". Thankfully though, one of the mentors came to my rescue. Ruth, a Director from another HMRC office, astutely observed that the thought of a project was leaving me somewhat nonplussed and she came up with a suggestion. I will never forget how the conversation went.

"John," she began, "have you ever thought of undertaking some kind of Diversity project?"

Somewhat stunned, I replied, "Ruth, I have not got a clue about Diversity."

Without frustration in her voice, she quickly responded, "But John don't you see, you are diverse. With your disability, your Christian faith and the fact of your age, you tick three of the Diversity boxes right away".

Clearly I had not seen it like that before and she suggested that I write a short talk on the premise of what makes me tick and make it available as a Diversity presentation for managers at their team meetings in our building.

Ruth went on, "As a manager myself, I can tell you they will snap your hands off because many of us, if we are honest, have not got much idea about what to do with Diversity, even though it is an agenda item at each meeting".

Ruth's enthusiasm for the project and her encouragement (there goes that word again!) gave me the necessary impetus to settle on the idea and get on with it. I therefore approached the idea with the same verve as I had with the article I had previously written for the office magazine, which had kicked all this off in the first place.

As *Breakthrough* drew to a conclusion, I had already written up the outline of my proposed Diversity presentation and to my surprise I was asked to showcase it at the final *Breakthrough* session. Though understandably a little nervous, I did feel unusually confident as I premiered *Fear, Fun and Faith* for the very first time.

This, my Diversity project, has since become an award-winning presentation shared across the country. My very first foray into the world of public speaking detailed my story about how I first became blind and what it felt like, some of the fears in my life before and after losing my sight, some of the funny anecdotes that I have accumulated over the years and how my faith has enabled me to overcome many challenges to allow me to go on to live a joyful, fulfilling life.

At the conclusion of my talk it was so heartening to hear spontaneous applause break out from my fellow delegates, mentors and trainers alike. I received the most glowing feedback and I returned to the typing pool feeling very well equipped and ready for the challenges that lay ahead. There was a new excitement now living within my heart and I wasted no time at all in sending an email to all managers in City Centre House, attaching the notes of my presentation and making myself available for any Diversity slot in future team meetings. Ruth was so right, within two or three days I had received about 20 invitations to speak at meetings around the building.

The first meeting was so memorable and was to set the tone for so many that were to follow. It was with our Business Support Team and their manager, Janet Wilkes, who was someone I met on my very first day working for the Inland Revenue way back in 1969. She was then an 18 year old clerical assistant and on many a cold day she would wear her Aston Villa scarf to work; many years later she and her husband are still season ticket holders at Villa Park just like me.

My slot was at 11.45am, the last 15 minute item on the agenda. *Fear, Fun and Faith* went down even better than I could have imagined and after finishing on time, not only did I receive a warm round of applause, but I was bombarded with a whole series of interesting and at times quite penetrating questions. After going over time by about 20 minutes, Janet said she would have to draw the meeting to a close because other people needed the room, however she turned to me and added;

"John, I think you have seriously underestimated the power of this presentation. You had people in tears and fits of laughter throughout and you can see by the amount of questions that you have really connected with people. I think you will need to consider extending your session to 30 or maybe 45 minutes to do it justice".

And with that the applause started all over again.

Other meetings went on in that vein for about two weeks and then there was a most interesting development. I was busy at my desk typing when I was visited by Alan, one of our other Directors. He said he had been travelling home on the train to Dudley, the previous evening when he had overheard a couple of lads talking animatedly about a presentation of mine they had attended earlier that day. Alan engaged them in conversation by asking them what so special about it. Apparently they said words to the effect of it being very inspirational, the best speech they have ever heard, that it should be compulsory listening for all staff and even made available on the NHS. Speechless, but encouraged and excited, I sat and listened as Alan continued, "On the basis of all the excellent feedback I am getting from people who have attended your talk, I wonder if you would be willing to come share *Fear, Fun and Faith* at our next Area Directors Board meeting to be held in Kettering?"

Of course I readily agreed and a fortnight later I was travelling with Alan in his car down to Kettering, a town I had visited once before many years earlier when we had lived in the Leicestershire town of Market Harborough, only about 20 miles away.

By now I had extended the presentation to 30 minutes and once again the response was the same. With a mixed audience of about 16 Directors from office across the country, I once again received prolonged applause and the added bonus for me was that these were leaders who had responsibility for many members of staff. Morale across the Civil Service was particularly low at this time with the Government needing to make substantial job cuts resulting in a great deal of uncertainty. It seemed like the time was just right for my positive upbeat presentation and within a very short time I was travelling to all of these HMRC offices and many more besides, receiving the same incredible responses.

I was travelling around the country by bus, train and taxi all by myself, which as a blind person, was something I had never done before without the company of my dear wife Sylvia there to accompany me. This was definitely a learning curve for me, but one which I thrived on as I saw it as a great adventure in the unknown.

One visit in particular stands out as it represented a unique challenge for me. I was to speak at an office meeting in East Kilbride and because of the length of the train journey I would have to stay overnight in a hotel. Never before had I had to face staying in a hotel alone before, let alone as a blind person. The train ride was fantastic, I boarded at Birmingham New Street and headed for Glasgow and the Virgin rail staff were so kind to me. The Guard frequently came and asked me if I needed the toilet or any refreshments and another member of staff took time out just to come and chat with me. They were so reassuring and when we actually arrived in Glasgow, one of them actually escorted me to the taxi.

The taxi driver was then most kind and saw me safely into the Holiday Inn reception and after checking in, I was assured by the Receptionist that if I needed anything at all, I only needed to dial zero on the phone by my bed and they would see to it. A very thoughtful Polish staff member took me to my room and gave me a guided tour around so that I knew where everything was located. The customer service was exemplary and I was beginning to feel so loved. Before leaving the room, the Polish gentleman said that at meal time he would come up and fetch me and take me to the dining room, where someone would look after me.

All was great, so with a feeling of smug satisfaction I rang home to let Sylvia know I had arrived safely and was doing fine. That done, I decided to visit the bathroom before doing a little unpacking. I found my way in to the bathroom suite fine but as I fumbled around for the cord and pulled it, I was horrified to hear the alarms go off. Instantly I realised I had pulled the wrong cord, although to be truthful I had no idea there was more than one anyway.

Within moments, my Polish friend returned and I immediately apologised profusely for my mistake. He would hear none of it, however, saying that it was his fault for not pointing it out and what I had done had in fact highlighted a breach in the security.

Having unpacked the few things I had and taken a little rest, it was soon time to go down for dinner. My friendly Pole duly arrived and the lovely aroma of steak and fish assailed my senses as we walked into the restaurant area. He sat me down at a table and within a moment or two, a waitress with a soft Scottish accent was at my side reading the menu. I decided on cod, chips and peas followed by apple pie and custard as I wanted something fairly simple to eat so I did not make a great mess on the table, or more embarrassingly perhaps, down my clothes.

After I had finished a most enjoyable meal, the waitress asked if I wanted to sit in the bar. Although I fancied going back to the safety of my room, not wishing to appear totally unsociable I agreed to go to the bar, where I requested a pint of John Smith's smooth beer, a drink I was introduced to by my brother Paul. In that 45 minutes or so I had a brief flirtation with what it must be like for single people all of the time. I sat there reflecting on my day and then secretly hoping someone would come over and begin to make conversation just to help the time pass a little quicker and take away the encroaching feeling of being alone. It was only a momentary feeling of isolation, but it was very real. Having finished my drink, a waiter came over to ask if I wanted another, but I politely declined and said I would like to go back to my room. I think my Polish friend had gone off home because now I was accompanied by another gentleman with a strange accent, who was again most kind and helpful.

After a contented night's sleep I was up, washed and ready for room service to collect me and take me down for breakfast. Once again, a lovely aroma greeted me and after smelling that bacon there was no way I could refuse the full English breakfast.

Later having gone back to my room, packed my bag and checked out, I was soon in a taxi and heading for the office to begin a series of three talks to different teams. Gary, the manager who had arranged the event, met me in reception and took me to the room where the first meeting was to be held. Within a few minutes I was being introduced in glowing terms to a very mixed audience numbering about 25 people. The manager explained in detail how

I as a blind person, had courageously made the journey from Birmingham the day before and stayed overnight at the Holiday Inn. He gave me a big, heroic build up and as I stood up to speak I sensed a wave of sympathy, maybe sadness, emanating from my audience.

I began by saying "Please don't feel sorry for me because I am one of the richest men in the world".

I went on to explain how since leaving Birmingham the previous day I had literally been deluged with so many expressions of loving kindness that my life had already been greatly enriched. I had their interest and for the next 45 minutes they listened with rapt attention, laughing in all the appropriate places.

In each of the three sessions in East Kilbride I experienced a warmth of friendship that was most touching and the feedback I received, particularly by email back in my Birmingham office, was some of the most encouraging I have ever had. One comment in particular will live with me forever although it did not come until about two weeks after the event. A manager of one of the teams I had spoken to said he had deliberately delayed giving his response because he wanted to see whether the amazing effects would die off. Happily they did not and he said, "Two weeks after attending the event, I am still buzzing. I feel as though a firework has gone off up my backside and blasted me out of my apathy". How about that for basic Glaswegian talk?

Back in the typing pool we began to get wind that redundancies were in the air as, quite honestly, typists were becoming an endangered species due to the fact that many people had excellent keyboard skills and were able to type their own letters and reports on their own computers. It was not long before the news came that our pool was to become extinct. Some of the people would take early retirement, whilst others decided to move on from the Civil Services. For myself, I was really surprised to be told that I along with another visually impaired colleague were going to be trained to undertake tax work. To be frank, this prospect did not thrill me at all. I would have loved to have continued making Diversity presentations on a full time basis, but clearly there was no official role for that kind of work, so it was that I began training to do what was then called Open Case clearance work.

As with a lot of things in life that we initially have misgivings about, it turned out to be pretty good. The trainers were fantastic people and there was a wonderful sense of pioneering as we were in the early stages of creating new jobs for visually impaired people in the future. I had always enjoyed my typing work, except when I could not understand the person dictating on tape that is! This new job, however, was a challenge and I loved the fact it was breaking new ground.

Since then I have learned, along with about 50 other visually impaired people across HMRC, to do a range of tax administration jobs within my pay band. By and large I have loved every minute of it, just as long as the technology works okay, which is not always the case of course. Requests for me to make my "Fear, Fun and Faith" presentation were still coming in at the rate of two or three a month when I received my first bit of recognition.

I have copied the paragraph below direct from the HMRC website;

"In November 2005, John was invited by Helen Ghosh, now Permanent Secretary at DEFRA, to represent the Department at the 'Race for Opportunities' dinner at the Park Lane Hotel in London, attended by representatives from 40 top UK companies.

The event recognised that John was one of nine people across the Department who had most advanced the cause of diversity and equality."

This was a very prestigious event and I got to stay overnight in the nearby Hilton Hotel with three of the other representatives from the Department. Those who know me are aware that I am not much of a suit kind of a person, I feel much more comfortable in smart casual attire. For this occasion, however, I thought I would need to purchase a decent suit and at this point one of life's little 'coincidences' took place.

I get quite a lot of those and someone recently observed that the more we pray the more of these, 'God incidences' as he called them seem to occur.

I recall it vividly now. I was crossing Poplar Road in Solihull and halfway across I heard a lady exclaim "Look, it's John". I hurried to the safety of the pavement and instinctively looked back. Two people were in front of me in a flash and introduced themselves. Debbie, worked for the Inland Revenue full time in the national Equality and Diversity team based in London and her husband Dave was a senior grade HM Inspector of Taxes, as they were called in those days. They had just moved to live in Solihull as Dave's job had brought them to the West Midlands.

Debbie began to congratulate me on being invited to the event in London, saying what an honour it was and so well deserved.

Dave chipped in, "I hope you have got your evening suit ready".

I told him I did not own a suit so would have to buy one. He then informed me that as I was attending as a representative of the

Inland Revenue, I could hire an evening suit and charge it to the Department.

"Get along to Moss Brothers, right now and get measured up. Any problems at work and refer them to me" he said firmly.

What a chance meeting that was. I did as I was 'commanded' and went along to Moss Brothers and got my suit sorted. I had great fun when I arrived home telling Sylvia and the rest of the family about my little adventure.

I am happy to say, all went okay. The local office were fine about the suit and my Park Lane adventure passed off very satisfyingly, though I did almost have to pinch myself once or twice on the realisation that I was mixing in such esteemed company. Again I have to say, people were really kind in guiding me, showing me around, taking me to the loo and helping cut up my food. I was glad to get out of my suit though and relax in to something more informal after the event

At this point, allow me to introduce you to Nick John, another Tax Inspector, who was to enter stage left and play a significant part in my life.

Chapter 3 - Nominations and new beginnings

I first came across Nick while I was in the typing pool. Nick's work was very interesting to type and his dictation was superb. His command of the English language was excellent as was his diction. Coming from Gloucester, he had a very distinctive West Country lilt to his voice also. One other thing caused Nick to stand out from the other people we typed for too and that was his courtesy. He would always begin each tape (now that takes you back doesn't it?) by saying "Good morning typist", or some other appropriate salutation and finish by saying, "Thank you and that is the end of the dictation". These may seem to be simple courtesies, but my, did they make you feel appreciated as a typist, and as a result, when Nick's work appeared in the tray there was a mad scramble to do it.

I remember writing to Nick to thank him for his work, for his courtesy and to say how much we all enjoyed working for him. I was then greatly heartened when Nick turned up as one of the mentors on the *Breakthrough* programme although I did not get much of an opportunity to interact with him though as he was chosen to mentor someone else. Nick was, however, in the audience when I premiered *Fear, Fun and Faith* at *Breakthrough* and he was one who responded very positively to that presentation. Some months later Nick invited me to give the talk to one of the teams he was managing and again he was most affirming of me.

I did know that Nick had gone through a very painful divorce and was bringing up his two young daughters by himself. Happily he had found love again with Jane, a fellow Tax Inspector. However tragedy was to strike because Jane was killed in a boating accident at the Stourport -on-Severn carnival.

I was devastated for my colleague and friend and sent him my prayers and condolences. After a few weeks had elapsed, I acted on my feelings and asked Nick if he would like to go for a coffee. At *Breakthrough* Nick had acquired a reputation of being a devotee of Starbucks, but actually on getting to know him, I found he was more of a 'Costa' man.

Anyway, we did meet for coffee on a two or three monthly basis and it was during one of these times Nick told me he had nominated me for a Civil Service Equality and Diversity award. I felt humbled, politely thanked him but thought no more of it. About two months or so had passed when on arriving at my desk one morning I began, as usual, checking my emails. There was one in particular which was out of the ordinary in that it came from The Cabinet Office. It appeared as though my nomination for an award had not only been successful, but I had got through to the finals to be held in London. An attachment to the email was my official invitation to attend the finals day to be held in London and at this point I can do no better than reproduce below the piece that appeared on the Civil Service website page at that time.

"The first ever Civil Service Diversity and Equality Awards took place on 26th October 2006 at Lancaster House, London. Timed to coincide with the first anniversary of the Diversity 10-Point Plan, the Awards recognised the outstanding achievements of civil servants at all levels in the field of diversity and equality excellence and celebrated our successes in policy, employment and service delivery. The awards were presented by Sir Gus O'Donnell, Cabinet Secretary and Head of the Home Civil Service. Bill Jeffrey, Civil Service Diversity Champion and Pat McFadden, Parliamentary Secretary for the Cabinet Office, also made short speeches. Over 170 entries were received from across all regions, departments and agencies and from a wide range of diversity and equality areas.

Congratulations to everyone who submitted an entry and especially to our finalists and winners for making the awards such a successful celebration of diversity and equality excellence and reinforcing our commitment to continuous improvement in this field."

I was allowed to take one other person with me and although I initially thought it would be Sylvia, she felt very strongly it should be Nick, as he was the one who had put forward such a convincing nomination on my behalf. Nick was really surprised when I asked him, but he was only too delighted to accompany me as a guide and a friend. I don't remember much about the journey on the train to London, other than feeling very excited. We arrived at Lancaster House, where we were served refreshments in the large entrance hall. After a short time of milling around we were ushered into the main room for the presentations, where we enjoyed a pleasant light lunch.

Over the meal, somehow I got involved in a discussion with Nick about faith and the existence of God. It so happened that I had just finished watching a four week series on BBC 1 called 'The Miracles of Jesus' presented by Rageh Omaar, very much known at the time as being 'The BBC's man in Baghdad' because he was often seen reporting from the war zone in Iraq. Anyway I had been mightily impacted by this documentary series and waxed lyrical to Nick about how impressed I had been by Rageh Omaar's total impartiality towards Jesus, given that he was coming from a background of Islam. I was in full swing enthusing about Rageh, when Nick tapped me on the knee and said;

"This is spooky and you are never going to believe it, but unless I am very much mistaken, Rageh Omaar is standing right behind you".

With that Nick arose from his seat and left me for a few moments. Shortly afterwards Nick came back and said,

"John, stand up, there is someone I would like you to meet".

I stood up and after shaking hands warmly I was engrossed in animated conversation with 'the BBC man from Baghdad'.

For the record, Rageh seemed a lovely guy and he said the series about Jesus was the most challenging he has ever had to undertake and it made a profound impression on him as he was forced to the conclusion that the 'miracles' of Jesus were actually true.

Soon afterwards Rageh was at the head of the room presenting the awards. When it came to the Outstanding Achievement category, the one for which I had been shortlisted, my heart began to race and thump quite loudly within me. The citation for each of the three finalists was read out. See mine below…

"John Flanner, of Her Majesty's Revenue and Customs, for single-handedly pioneering a series of talks about his experiences as a blind person. HM Revenue and Customs (HMRC) was formed on 18th April 2005 and has responsibility for collecting and administering taxes and other duties. John is a member of the Open Case Team of HMRC.

Following a personal development programme, Breakthrough, John single-handedly pioneered a series of inspirational talks about his experiences as a blind person. Staff who have attended his talks have found his presentation, about how he went from a fully sighted person to losing his sight suddenly at the age of 19, engaging, humorous and inspiring. Through his talks, John has led to many staff, including top management, changing their perceptions about disabilities. He has been a great inspiration and role model."

"The judges were similarly moved and inspired by John's ability and courage in overcoming obstacles such as learning to cope so effectively with his own disability, as well as his experience of personal loss whilst continuing his persuasive promotional work on diversity. Countless testimonials including feedback via e-mails and phone calls, show that John has continuously inspired and motivated others. John also shows outstanding pride and passion in his work, both in his commitment to his 'day job' and in his mission to engage people in diversity issues. He is undoubtedly a role model and a deserved finalist of a special award recognising outstanding achievement."

Once the citations had been read, the fanfare sounded and the MC was heard to say these now legendary words "and the winner is…" Those few moments of silence sounded like an eternity, but then the words came… "John Flanner".

A quick tap on the shoulder from Nick and he was leading me to the front to pick up my award from Sir Gus O'Donnell and a hearty handshake from the man who now felt like my old friend, Rageh Omaar.

It was an awesome and surreal few moments as I posed for photographs. I could not wait to get outside and phone Sylvia to let her know. For the record I actually received a certificate and an engraved crystal paperweight. My dear wife does not collect much, but she does like crystal, so I thought she would be pleased with that.

The Awards ceremony gave me an opportunity to meet up with the man who at the time was CEO of HMRC, Paul Gray. We enjoyed a really easy conversation for about 10 minutes in which Paul said my presentation was all the more poignant because it came from the grass roots of the organisation and not from a senior manager. He said, in his experience it was unique that someone from my grade should make an impact across all levels of the Department. Paul went on to say that he would like to see me being properly remunerated for the valuable work I was undertaking and he would instruct one of his Board members to be in touch with me to discuss that.

"My goodness," I thought, "this day is just getting better and better".

True to his word, a week or two later, I received a phone call from Chris Hopson, then one of the Senior Board members, to go to London and meet with him, along with someone from Equality and Diversity, to discuss my future work and career. Now this was getting exciting, I thought to myself.

Then something happened on a national level, that you would never have believed would have affected me, but it most surely did.

The story broke in the Press that some Child Benefit discs had gone missing, containing thousands of pieces of personal data. As always happens in such scandals, there was a call for heads to roll and within a few days, Paul Gray, the man at the top of our organisation, had resigned and with him went my hopes for a lucrative promotion.

Following this turn of events, attitudes towards me did change. I did go to London and meet with Chris together with another Diversity colleague and indeed a salary of £32,000 was discussed. To satisfy HR requirements, a job description was written for the job I had created and I was interviewed in London for the position of Staff Engagement Support Officer. Strangely I did not get the job and when I requested feedback, I was told it was because I lacked experience in delivering messages at a senior level. Shortly afterwards the job was totally withdrawn. Mysteriously, it all went quiet after that and a lot of the people in senior management nationally moved on.

I would be lying to say this was not desperately disappointing, even hurtful and confusing. Many people locally were at a loss to know what had gone on. Some even suggested that I did not get the job because I was too open about my Christian faith.

I was still enjoying my regular job though and due to me winning the Civil Service award, this brought me to the attention of people in other Departments. It was not long before I began receiving invitations to speak at team meetings in the Home Office, Cabinet Office, Ministry of Justice and Veterinary Laboratories Agency to name just a few. It was a fabulous experience for me and I became quite a regular visitor to Westminster, catching the Chiltern train from Solihull to Marylebone. I love that little London station, always finding the staff there so helpful and kind.

It was at a Cabinet Office event that I heard a speaker who was to have a profound effect upon me and help influence many of my presentations in the future. The event was a day conference held at Somerset House to celebrate the role the Christian Faith had played in shaping the Civil Service in Britain. The Conference was opened up by Sir Gus O'Donnell as, the then head of the Civil Service and one of the other speakers was Stephen Timms MP.

Both men were good in their own right, but the man who really captured my attention was Chan Abraham. He is a businessman and church pastor, as well as CEO of the Luminus Group of companies, who I understand seek to provide affordable and accessible housing for people on low incomes in and around the Huntingdon area of England.

I was gripped by Chan's overall passion for people as well as his faith of course, which was clearly his driving force. Chan said he had come to the UK from Sri Lanka and had been horrified to find that a great many people in the UK live, what he called a Monday to Friday death, just living for the weekend. He found that attitude to be quite appalling and set about changing that culture within his company.

Chan obviously succeeded because he told us that for several years his company had won awards for being one of the best firms to work for in the UK and I am not surprised for in that moment I wanted to work for him too. Suffice to say though, I have been on a mission ever since to try and impact people with the same passion and enthusiasm for work which Chan imparted to me on that memorable day.

Chapter 4 - Achieving the impossible

Since commencing my talks I had always encouraged people to write to me giving reaction to my presentation. I invited people to comment on what had helped or inspired them, what I could do to improve performance and content as well as any constructive criticism.

I have received hundreds of responses and some of the stories were most touching and it quickly became apparent that *Fear, Fun and Faith* was connecting with people at many different levels. One lady wrote to say that she had been dragged 'kicking and screaming' into my meeting, but had been so inspired she had decided to call the baby she was pregnant with Faith – yes she knew it was a girl! A few months later I received a further email to tell me how well Faith was doing and how beautiful she was.

Someone else wrote to say how listening to me gave her hope for the future after she had found out that one of her children may go blind because of a defective gene. Then again a man wrote to me saying that hearing my talk was such a tonic; it was only his second day back at work after several months off with depression and it had been many years since he had laughed so much.

In more than a hundred of the emails I received, however, there was a common theme.

"John you must write a book" is what they were all saying. "You have so many stories to tell and it is important that more people are inspired by your story".

With that powerful encouragement ringing in my ears, I sat down at my home computer one Easter weekend and began to pour my heart out as I expanded on the themes of *Fear, Fun and Faith*. I am not a trained writer and I do not consider myself as a professional, but I am passionate and enthusiastic and I just write down what I am feeling.

Thinking back to *Breakthrough* for a moment when it came to writing down our goals and aspirations for the future, I said to my mentor, "One day I want to write a book". I felt at that point of my life I had encountered such a rich diversity of experiences, I just wanted to pass on some of those life lessons for the interest and benefit of others. I made a start, and the constant flow of encouraging emails simply kept fuelling the fire of enthusiasm for the project. In all it took me about a year to complete my first book as I did most of my writing during the late nights and early mornings while Sylvia was working night shifts as an Health Care Assistant at the Marie Curie Hospice in Solihull.

After our children had all grown up and left home, Sylvia commenced work as a care assistant. To begin with she looked after a few people in their own homes before starting work in an old people's residential home. After a year or two she moved on to working in a nursing home and gained more skills. She really did love her work and developed a reputation as a high class carer. While working at the Prince of Wales Nursing Home in the Solihull Lodge area of Birmingham, the Matron Anne Barry observed that Sylvia had a particular level of skill and compassion with people who were close to death. Although not wishing to lose Sylvia, Anne did encourage her to keep her eyes open for suitable work in the hospice field.

There was a hospice quite near to where we were living so Sylvia actually dropped in a copy of her CV to the office and to her great surprise she received a phone call within two weeks inviting her to an interview.

The interview went well and Sylvia was offered a position as a Health Care Assistant working 30 hours per week. Although nervous to begin with, Sylvia took to the work like the proverbial duck to water.

It was not long before the harsh realities of such work were hitting us right between the eyes, or perhaps deep in the heart would be a better expression. Very early in Sylvia's new career she found herself nursing a very glamorous young lady in her late twenties. Tracy had been a manager at River Island, but now had terminal cancer. Sylvia lost her heart to this lovely young woman and when she died it was heart-breaking all around. We attended her funeral and I will never forget being encouraged to dance in the pews to a Bob Marley song as a fitting tribute to this vivacious and beautiful person who had been lost to this world far too soon.

Sylvia managed the emotional side of this work pretty well for most of the time, but it was when young people came in that it affected her the most. Day after day when she came home from work we shared stories, humorous and otherwise about patients, their relatives and staff. It was the kind of job where it was needful to talk to get things off your chest and we often spent time lifting people up to God in prayer.

For me, it was a real eye-opener to realise that hospice life was not all depressing, far from it in fact for they had a lot of fun too. Also I came to understand that not everyone who goes into a hospice actually dies there, many go in just to get their pain levels under control and then they go home. The truth is that whilst there were many sad stories, there was an incredible amount of fun and laughter as well.

I was really proud of Sylvia and her colleagues at the Warren Pearl, Marie Curie Hospice. The levels of compassion shown to residents was deeply touching, the fund-raising events were truly legendary and the multitude of ways in which they put a smile on the faces of patients and their families was highly innovative.

There was one particular idea which Sylvia asked me to get involved in. They had a terminally ill patient, Ron, a very keen Birmingham City football supporter who was upset that he would probably never get to see his beloved team again. Sylvia asked me to write to the then Club manager, Steve Bruce, to highlight the situation and see if one of the players could visit the hospice.

I wrote the letter and a few days later one of the nurses on duty at the hospice took a call from Birmingham City Football Club to say that two of the players had just left training and would be visiting the hospice that afternoon. Later in the day Paul Devlin and Curtis Woodhouse (later to become a successful professional boxer) arrived, bringing with them a signed first team shirt.

Ron was overwhelmed with joy at seeing two of his heroes in person and he had great pleasure in having his photograph taken with the players, plus others members of his family while wearing the shirt. A couple of days later Ron sadly passed away, but the local newspaper covered the story with the headline 'My Blue Heaven for Dying Blues Fan', showing a photograph taken at the hospice of Ron posing in his Blues shirt alongside the two players. A quote from the brother in the article said that this was one of the happiest days of Ron's life. Such a simple act, yet it brought so much pleasure to a hurting family.

With Sylvia working in such a highly emotive environment, my interest was aroused as to the origins of the hospice movement and this curiosity led me to discover its founder, Dame Cicely Saunders. The more research I did the more I became inspired by this great lady. As an avid letter-writer myself (now more emails than snail mail!), one of the hooks that drew me in was the fact that Cicely wrote so many letters to the British Government as she campaigned for palliative care to be officially recognised and for finances to be released to set up the first hospice. I reliably understand that she wrote thousands of letters in support of her ideas, time and time again overcoming the disappointment of so many rejection letters, until eventually the breakthrough came.

I can do no better by way of a tribute than reproduce the article taken from the St Christopher's Hospice website in the appendices at the back of this book with their kind permission. I am thrilled to say that because of Sylvia's employment with Marie Curie, we were honoured to be able to attend the memorial service at Westminster Abbey. For many years Sylvia had faithfully supported me in a whole host of innovative endeavours, but now it was my turn to get behind her in a job that she was not only passionate about, but also very good indeed.

It was while Sylvia was working in this field of care that she first experienced health difficulties. On what I thought would be a pretty typical day I left for work by taxi at about 6.30am, leaving Sylvia to leave the house and drive the 10 minutes to Warren Pearl a few minutes later. How wrong could I have been for this was to be no ordinary day.

Just after lunch my desk phone began to ring and taking off my headphones quickly, I picked up the receiver.

"Hello, John speaking, can I help you?" I enquired.

"John, it's me Sylvie, I need you to come home," she said faintly, "I am very confused and I have a bad headache".

By this time her speech became quite slurred and filled with concern, I said, "I will get a taxi home right away".

In no time at all I was on my way to a taxi, pausing along the way to ring my son Ian, who would in all probability be working nearer to our home. Sure enough he was and in fact he arrived at the house just before me.

We found Sylvia in a bit of a state. She did manage to say that she had been to work, but as she had a very bad headache, the nurse in charge had sent her home. She could not remember driving home and by now she was talking fairly unintelligibly in riddles. Phrases like 'ear infection' and 'antibiotics' were some of the repetitive things we could understand. Quickly I rang 999 and within a few minutes the paramedics had arrived and were conducting all kinds of tests on Sylvia, who was still protesting that all she needed was antibiotics for her bad ear.

Under a certain amount of protestation, Sylvia was taken by ambulance to Solihull Hospital with Ian and myself following by car. After the initial administration work had been done we were left waiting along with several other people for what seemed like an eternity. It was made all the worse because Sylvia was clearly in distress with a lot of pain and confusion and to our acute embarrassment she kept on shouting out and swearing because nothing seemed to be happening. This also convinced us of course that something was seriously wrong as this was so unlike Sylvia, behaving like that.

In truth it was about 90 minutes before we saw a Doctor and after looking into Sylvia's ears, he proclaimed her to be suffering from an ear infection and he prescribed antibiotics and painkillers. Sylvia seemed to take quite a delight in saying "I told you so."

Going home in the car, however, Sylvia was still very confused and even said to Ian, "Why are you driving when you can't see? Let your Dad drive".

When back home we put Sylvia to bed, making sure she had taken her medication.

Downstairs I said to Ian, "I am not happy and I am going to ring Gordon".

Dr Gordon Coleman is a long-standing family friend. Gordon and his wife Julia have four kids, just like us and many years before we used to go on holidays together. We have some brilliant memories of those times spent in places like Wales, Devon and Cornwall with the Coleman's. Gordon's parents in fact had been medical missionaries in Iran for many years and had in fact been held hostage back in the early 1980's. They were among a number of such hostages whose release was secured by the Archbishop of Canterbury's Special Envoy, Terry Waite. All of that of course was International news at the time and we were much involved in praying for the family during those difficult, testing days.

Now this was a testing day for us and Gordon was the friend I was turning to. As soon as I described the symptoms, Gordon immediately said I should go and wake Sylvia up as she needed to be admitted to Heartlands Hospital for a brain scan.

Foolishly in hindsight I said, "Can't it wait until morning? Sylvia will be really angry with me if I wake her now".

Gordon's wise reply will live with me for the rest of my life.

"Better for her to be angry with you for half an hour now than you live with a lifetime of regret".

I got the message immediately and quickly went upstairs with Ian to wake Sylvia and tell her an ambulance was on its way to take her to hospital for a scan.

Of course she was not at all pleased with this, but in no time at all we were blue-lighted to Heartlands Hospital, where Sylvia did undergo a brain scan. Ian persuaded me to go home and get some rest after that and he would sit with his Mum until morning. I came home and went straight to my computer to begin emailing many of my contacts requesting prayer for my wife, who I realised was seriously ill.

On returning to the hospital next morning I was told that Sylvia was having a bleed in the brain and she would be transferred to the Queen Elizabeth Hospital for surgery. Later in the day we were again blue-lighted by ambulance across the city to the Queen Elizabeth Hospital (QE) and I vividly recall Sylvia having a very lucid conversation in the ambulance with the South African paramedic about cricket.

When safely ensconced in her bed at the QE, Sylvia was wired up to a variety of drips, one of which, we were told, was to sedate her as it was important that she was kept quiet and still. During the night she would be under close supervision on the High Dependency Unit, while Doctors made a decision as to the right course of treatment.

On the way home from the hospital that night Ian and I along with our daughter Beverley, who had arrived from her home in Hampshire, decided to stop off for a pizza. On the window of *Big John's* there was a notice indicating that they had just launched their brand new giant pizza, which just happened to be called Big Mama's Back. If you are anything like me, when you are in a tight spot you will cling on to any sign of encouragement. I, only half-jokingly, took this as a prophetic sign that Sylvia was going to get well and that very soon we would be saying "Mama's back" – notice I dropped the 'Big' though. It did bring a bit of light relief into what had been a very heavy couple of days. The Big Mama's Back Pizza did turn out to be rather delicious too.

Back at the hospital, as a daily routine a nurse or doctor would come and ask Sylvia simple questions such as "What is your date of birth?", "What is your address?", or "How many children do you have?". This was both sad and humorous at times, as when asked her age, Sylvia said "I am 21, or is it 76…. I am not quite sure". Other simple questions also flummoxed her, but she did not get any of the teasers about the Royal family wrong. She certainly knew the name of the Queen and all of her children.

In all Sylvia was in hospital for nearly three weeks, but the wonderful thing was that she did not have to have an operation on her brain in the end as we were told the fabulous news that the bleeding had stopped of its own accord. Whilst this does happen from time to time, we could not help but think that just maybe all of those prayers had helped too. I had great delight in sending follow up emails to the many people I knew who had been praying.

When Sylvia was eventually discharged, I will never forget her absolute joy as she marvelled at the simple things she saw during the car journey home. Not far from the Queen Elizabeth Hospital is the Edgbaston cricket ground where we have enjoyed many happy summer days watching Warwickshire or England play cricket and Sylvia seemed particularly excited to see the outside of the stadium again. She was in awe of the beautiful blue sky, the flowers and the trees in gardens as we passed through Moseley and the busy streets of Shirley and Solihull. Like many people who have come close to death and then been given another chance as it were, she simply marvelled at the many things we all take for granted every day. Once home Sylvia then began about six months of convalescence before even contemplating going back to work at Marie Curie.

Sylvia did eventually return to work part-time, but in truth the stroke she had suffered had taken away quite a bit of her confidence and once she reached her 60th birthday we agreed this would be an ideal time for her to finish. It was a really hard decision for her to make because she genuinely loved her work with the patients and their families. Sylvia knew it was a great privilege to be able to do such a job and she did not give it up lightly. It was hard for her, but she did know beyond a shadow of a doubt, that this was the right time.

While all of this had been going on with Sylvia, there had been an interesting development regarding my *Fear, Fun and Faith* book. A considerable amount of time had elapsed since I had finished typing the original manuscript, got it proofread and edited by my friend John Cheek, and I then struggled considerably when it came to finding a willing publisher. In truth it was all a bit of a minefield, then, as so often happens, God seemed to place the right people at the right time in my path.

Philip and Dee Allen were fairly recent attendees at King's Church in Solihull where Sylvia and I had been members for nearly 10 years. Graham Pearce, a close friend and one of our church Elders said he thought it would be very beneficial for me to meet up with Philip and Dee sometime soon. Consequently we did meet on several occasions and I enjoyed their company very much indeed.

They were very highly motivated business people with interesting stories in their own right and they also had a background in public speaking and publishing. Philip in particular had been an agent at one time representing many well-known, inspirational speakers.

When he saw the kind of feedback I was receiving from my talks he tried hard to motivate me to 'up my game', leave HMRC and begin a new life as a professional motivational speaker. He talked to me very strongly in business language trying to help me see that I was worth far more than HMRC were prepared to pay me. He and Dee also strongly encouraged me to self-publish *Fear, Fun and Faith,* the book, stating that if I was still going around making *Fear, Fun and Faith* presentations within the Civil Service, then I would need to have a product I could offer people afterwards. Dee had already self-published a couple of books by her father, so she took it on board to get my book published and that is exactly what she did. I will always be so grateful to both Philip and Dee for the help they gave me at that time. Their stay in Solihull was pretty brief and before long they moved out to Cheltenham and it seems like they came into my life, like so many over the years, for that particular season so that we could mutually encourage one another.

I cannot tell you just how thrilled I was to get the first two copies of the book in my hands. It was such a proud moment and I could not help but reminisce back to a time almost 50 years earlier when I sat in front of my careers officer at school.

"Well John", he said, "what do you want to do with your life?"

"I want to be a writer," I replied, "reporting on football and cricket".

I will never forget what he said in response…"Oh! That's good, I don't get many of those".

He then went on to explain all of the studying I would need to do and the qualifications I would need to achieve. My heart sank at his words, believing I was not clever enough to do that, so I gave up on my dream and when I left school a few months later, my Dad got me a job as an office junior in an Architects' office at Fort Dunlop in Birmingham.

As a teenager attending football matches, mainly Aston Villa I have to say, I would often write a report on the game I had just seen. I would then compare my report with the one in the Sunday newspaper and I would conclude that mine was a more accurate description of the match and that gave rise to my desire. "What fun", I thought to myself, "actually being paid to watch and write about a sport that you love". It was not to be, however, the careers officer's words had seen to that.

As I hold *Fear, Fun and Faith* in my hand in the present day, I realised I could have done it after all. I did have the ability to write and all it needed was encouragement and lots of it at that. Never should we underestimate the power of encouragement. As the word denotes it is all about putting courage into people. It is still incredible to me to think that I have needed so many affirming words to be spoken over me in order for my potential as a writer and public speaker to begin to be realised. I truly believe that every person on the planet is born with tremendous gifts and potential. I actually agree with the Bible, which states that we are created in the image and likeness of God and irrespective of whether we believe or not, my conviction is that the gifts, talents and abilities are still there within each one of us.

Chapter 5 - Feedback and faith

Some children are very fortunate to be born into families where the parents are very together, supportive and affirming from the cradle to the grave as it were. In such circumstances, children are far more likely to grow up achieving their dreams and fulfilling their potential than those who are born into dysfunctional families where there is emotional trauma strife and constant criticism. My upbringing was not a bad one at all, but I still lacked any form of self-confidence and it has truly amazed me just how much I have needed in the way of encouragement and affirmation in order to be able to pursue what I am now doing at the age of 68. Better late than never though eh?

The book launch took place at The Bridge, home of Solihull Christian Fellowship (SCF) on the main Stratford Road in Shirley. The building is a modern facility, which enables this fine church to fulfil its purpose in serving the community. Having been a church member there and also a serving Elder, I know first-hand what a warm and friendly welcome awaits people as they walk through the doors of SCF.

The format of the evening was quite simple in that a few people who knew me well, said some nice things about me. I guess I was fortunate because we only usually get to hear those kind of eulogies at funerals and we say to one another afterwards "Pity they were not alive to hear that". Well I was very much alive and it was uplifting to hear what different people from the likes of work, church and family actually did think about me, or at least my strengths at any rate.

After a short interval for some light refreshments, I was then brought to the microphone so that I could actually make the *Fear,*

Fun and Faith presentation. People were then invited to join an orderly queue to purchase the book if they so wished. I sat at a table to sign the books if that was what people wanted, which thankfully, was what most people did. I had never signed my name so much in all of my life. Since going blind 45 years or so earlier, I had only ever had to sign my name on very few occasions on cheques or forms, but certainly not much else. It was clear then and still is now, that I am in need of some handwriting practice.

Since the publication of *Fear, Fun and Faith*, the book, one of the most exciting things has been to read feedback from people who have benefitted in a variety of ways from reading it. Below are just a few that particularly thrill me;

"I wish I had read your book 10 years ago as it may well have spared me a marriage from hell."
Rakesh, Southend-on-Sea

"I thought I was an atheist, but having read your book, I don't think I am."
David, Leeds

"I lead a support group for fibromyalgia suffers and as many of us experience depression, your sister gave me a copy of your book. I have to say I have not read a book in many years, but I could not put Fear, Fun and Faith down. It may me laugh and cry in equal measure and I cannot thank you enough."
Sue, Walsall

"I want to tell you of something exciting that happened in my house this last weekend. You have brought laughter back into our home. I was downstairs making an early morning cup of tea, when suddenly I was startled to hear my husband Mark laughing upstairs. Nothing strange in that you may think, but Mark had not

laughed for a long time. He had been on long term sick leave suffering from M.E. and related depression. I could not wait to take the tea back upstairs to find out what had caused this outburst of hilarity. As I entered the bedroom I asked what had got into him and Mark said that he was intrigued to know what I had had my head stuck in all weekend so he had reached out in curiosity and picked up Fear, Fun and Faith, beginning to read at the Fun section. He then began to read to me the wallpaper and other stories. It was so exciting hearing Mark laugh again and I want to thank you for writing the book and bringing the sunshine back into our lives."
Lorraine, Croydon

I have already made fleeting references to two churches, which is not surprising really because being an active member of a local church congregation has been important to Sylvia and me for the entirety of our married life. My love affair with the church began way back at the age of 21, two years after going blind, when I met my typing teacher Mrs. Craig at the residential course in Pembridge Place, Notting Hill, London. One day she spoke to me about her Christian faith, which did not threaten me, because I thought I was a Christian; after all I had been born in England, christened as a baby and lived a decent sort of a life. The way Mrs. Craig spoke though made it appear as if it was actually possible to know God in a personal way. To be honest, at that stage of my life I did not know for sure that God existed, but I did say my prayers at night most of the time as a bit of an insurance policy just in case he was there.

Sensing that I was not totally disinterested, Mrs. Craig introduced me to a young blind married couple named Tony and Margaret Abbot, who were themselves Christians and attended Westminster Chapel. At the conclusion of a weekend where I stayed with Tony and Margaret at their flat in Acton, I decided, somewhat nervously to attend the Sunday evening service at Westminster Chapel. I had no idea this was one of the UK's most famous Churches, nor that the evening in question, would be so life-transforming for me.

Without going into every detail of that service, I can say I found the atmosphere to be really inspiring. There is something really uplifting about being part of a great crowd singing their songs of praise and worship; just ask football fans as they sing *Abide With Me* at the FA Cup Final, rugby fans as they sing their countries national anthems and people who have attended the last night of the proms. It was that kind of an aura for me at Westminster Chapel that night.

Now, nearly half a century on, I can still remember what the preacher spoke about during his sermon. He talked from the book of Ruth in the bible which is a brilliant little love story that would make a great movie. The preacher set the story into its historical context and then applied it in a modern way, explaining that Jesus himself came as the lover in the story to win back (the biblical word is redeem), the people he had created who had gone astray. I did not necessarily think I had gone astray but the service left me feeling that I wanted to get to know this Jesus in a personal way, just as my typing teacher appeared to.

After the service while mingling with a few people and sipping a hot cup of coffee, I was quietly mulling things over in my mind.

"I want to believe," I thought to myself, "but I do not want to be taken in".

Just then I got into conversation with a guy by the name of Mark, one of the youth workers in the church at the time. I remember clearly saying to him, "If you could prove to me that Jesus is now alive, I would believe".

The main entrance to Bitzaro Palace, Zante.

Our favourite place to stop for an ice cream whilst in Zante.

Sylvia and I five days before we flew out to Zante.

A selection of the many cards and flowers received by Sylvia following her stroke.

The main entrance to our church, Renewal Christian Centre, Lode Lane, Solihull.

WE are the CHURCH in the HEART OF THE NATION REACHING OUR COMMUNITY and our WORLD

Renewal's inspirational church vision statement on the wall in their foyer.

Outside Buckingham Palace after receiving my MBE on 13th February 2015.

Celebrating being on Her Majesty the Queen's Honours List with our family outside Buckingham Palace.

Meeting my hero Peter McParland MBE outside Wembley Stadium before the FA Cup Final, 2015.

'Refired not retired' - the next chapter of my career as a motivational speaker.

I will never forget his disappointing, but in hindsight wise answer.

Mark said, "I cannot prove to you that Jesus is alive, neither can I prove to you that I love my wife. If, however, you were to come and live with us for a month, hopefully you would deduce "Yes, Mark does love his wife" because you will have experienced love at work in our home."

That made sense to me, so I followed up by saying, "So what do I have to do then?"

Mark explained that if I were to pray, asking Jesus to come into my life and make himself real to me then he would do so and the proof of the pudding would be that in a month's time, my life would be different.

Put like that it was a win-win situation so I did pray a faltering prayer with Mark's guidance. At the sound of my "Amen" it seemed like loads of people were thronging around me offering hugs, handshakes and congratulations. At that moment it certainly felt as if I had made the right decision and in all the years since then I have hardly had any doubts.

Since then my journey through life has taken me to lots of different local churches from a range of traditions. Sylvia and I have been part of Anglican, Brethren, Pentecostal, House Church and modern charismatic groups right up to where we are now with the Free Methodist Church. We have received lots of good stuff in all the churches we have been part of and dare I say, given a lot into also in terms of time, talent and finance.

I understand there are a couple of thousand different Christian denominations in the world and I do wonder at times if this is confusing for people. Poor comparison I know, but I think of fizzy pop and all of the different flavours. There is orangeade, lemonade, limeade, cherryade, dandelion and burdock, cola etc. The fact is they are all flavours of pop enjoyed by some but not by others.

Many people too of course say "Well you don't have to go to church to be a Christian".

That is true to an extent, but I would say, if you are a sincere Christian, who is seeking to grow in your faith and your love for God then surely you would want to be part of a local community of believers so that you can work out your life together.

As an Aston Villa supporter I get the greatest buzz when I attend the games and shout for the team with my fellow Villa fans. Also as a bit of a movie buff I am not one for waiting for the DVD when a new film comes out. I want to be there at the cinema to enter into the total experiences of sound and vision. As we said before with the singing, there is a great dynamic which is created when people of like mind meet together.

Not long after *Fear, Fun and Faith* had been published I came home one Sunday night after I had been preaching at New Life Community Church in Rochdale.

After unpacking my bags and enjoying a refreshing mug of tea, Sylvia said, "Sit down I have something to say that is going to shock you".

She went on to explain that at church that morning it had been explained that the church was going to be changing in the sense that a new leader was going to be installed and the church would be taking on a different style. The congregation was told that because this was coming as a shock, there would be a period of three weeks grace, during which time we should all prayerfully consider whether we wanted to be committed to the new set up, or leave to find alternative places to worship locally.

This did come as a bolt out of the blue to some, like us, though others who were more in the know as it were, were not surprised. Initially we did not know what to do, but things did become clearer as the days and weeks passed.

First thing to say was that the new leader, Rob Davey had been with us for a year or so and we had grown to love and appreciate him and his wife and children. The determining factor for us though was that our friends and previous Elders, Graham and Paul had decided, it was time to move on. Sylvia concluded that only a few months before she had been laid up in hospital with her life hanging in the balance and it was the long friendship we had with Graham and Paul along with their wives that we had been able to call on. In light of that feeling of vulnerability we decided therefore to leave along with our friends and seek pastures anew.

I would like to say that our previous church has now re-emerged as Jubilee Church, part of Newfrontiers in Solihull and is doing a fine job. Many of our friends in fact are still there and we are in touch often. As for us, in all about 20 of us moved out and for a time we did meet together in homes as well as the local Women's Institute building for about a year. We met for prayer, worship, bible teaching and to specifically ask God if he was calling us to establish a new congregation in the area. Whilst I think we would all have liked that to be the case, God did not give his approval to start something else new in the area.

Within walking distance of where we live, there is a big church congregation, of which we have been aware for many years.

Indeed we have personally known the Senior Pastor, David Carr and his wife Molly, since they first started up with three or four people back in 1972. In those days David was a raw evangelist who used to visit our young people's church group as a singer with his band called *The Second Advent*. I was still a very young Christian, but I was excited by David's passion for God when he spoke between the songs.

Our biggest challenge when starting to attend Renewal Christian Centre was to cope with the enormity of the congregation. Well over 1,000 committed members, or partners, as they are called at Renewal. Early on though, maybe our second or third visit, a couple by the name of Richard and Barbara invited us to their home for a meal as part of their small home group.

We attended on the Wednesday night from 7pm to 9pm, enjoying a very nice lasagne around the table with about six other people, just chatting and getting to know each other. The evening concluded with a short discussion and prayers for personal needs. We only met once a month but out of those meetings some highly valued firm friendships have grown. We also decided to attend one of the church prayer meetings one Friday night from 8pm until midnight. People were so friendly and through that we have become firm friends with some Nigerian people through whom we are learning a lot about fervent prayer.

After about a year of being at Renewal we decided this is where God wanted us to put down our roots and so we committed to becoming Partners, which basically means we commit out time, our effort and our finances into getting behind the vision of the church. Renewal describes itself as being 'The Church in the Heart of the Nation reaching out to its Community and the World'.

We have learned that those are not just words on a mission statement but they are fleshed out every day as the church reaches out to people in need of food via the Helping Hands ministry, people with addiction issues through Opengate, debt counselling and money advice, support for marriages, people with mental health issues and so on. Week after week we hear of people's lives being dramatically transformed by the power of God's word along with frequent testimonies of people being miraculously healed.

Additionally, another facet of Renewal is Renewal Global which is the international arm of the church. Renewal Global is committed to planting new churches overseas as well as supporting Christians living in areas of the world where they are persecuted for their faith and contributing generously to places where natural disasters have taken place or people suffer as a result of terrorism. The church is far from perfect as any of the leaders will be quick to tell you, but it is clearly scratching where people are itching and meeting needs in the way I believe Jesus would do if he walked physically with us now.

Before moving on from the subject of Renewal Christian Centre, there are two other aspects I would like to chat with you about. Firstly to say, the building we meet in is an amazing facility that to me just oozes class. People who have lived in Solihull for many years will remember the site as being that of Wilsdons Coach Builders. Now, since Renewal acquired it, the building has been totally transformed in the same way that hundreds of lives have been. Sylvia and I have not been part of a church that has had its own building for many years, so this is a real treat for us. To worship God in an auditorium that holds around 800 people comfortably – we have three services now on Sunday to accommodate all who want to attend – is an awesome experience.

In addition there are many other rooms to accommodate staff, mother and toddler groups, a family centre, a large area for storing food for the poor and needy as well as the very attractively-priced Renewal Coffee Shop. I know I have missed out lots more besides, but suffice to say the Church leaders and partners have pulled out all the stops in terms of prayer and financial commitment not only to put this into place, but also to keep it up and running at such a standard of excellent.

From a purely personal point of view too I would add that the Pelican crossings outside the Church are as a direct result of a campaign I undertook way back in 1984. Our three daughters, Beverley, Sara and Allison all attended the school across the road from what was then the coach building factory.

Over the years there had been a number of minor accidents with children crossing the busy Lode Lane when coming out of school, eager to get home. At one particular point I felt I should head up a community campaign to get some kind of crossings outside of the school, but despite the nagging thought, I kept on putting it off. Then one day one of my own children was knocked over in the middle of the road when she was leaving school. Allison admitted she was rushing home as that day we had our first budgerigar, who we named Chico as he was a lovely yellow. Anyway Allison lay injured in the middle of the busy road having suffered a broken ankle and collapsed lung.

I needed no more provocation than this and I quickly began collecting signatures from people on Damsonwood, the housing estate where we still live, despite a four year break trying out life in Cornwall. I also enlisted the support of the staff at Lode Heath School, of whom the Head Teacher, Mr Evans, was a great support. Anyway it was a massive disappointment to find that our first application was turned down by the Solihull Council. On advice, though, we took it to an appeal and won it so eventually what we as a family at any rate fondly called *'The Allison Crossings'* were in place in a very short space of time. It was so heartening to do something for the community and to be safe in the knowledge that generations of schoolchildren from then on would be able to cross that busy road in total safety. The icing on the cake is that many years later when Renewal opened up instead of the coach company, the crossings now regularly assist thousands of worshippers to get into one of the fastest growing churches in the UK safe and sound.

Finally in this section I cannot resist giving a hearty recommendation to the autobiographical book written by our Senior Pastor, David Carr. It really is a most compelling read with something for everyone.   David came from most humble beginnings in Birmingham and suffered in his early years from a poor education, later discovering that much of that was due to him suffering from dyslexia.   David gives a very humorous and moving account of his childhood and growth into adulthood. He once worked as a bouncer before eventually transitioning and becoming a very successful businessman. Indeed at one point he handled the finances and pensions for over 500 top professional footballers and managers, including the likes of Brian Robson and Brian Clough. All this while trying to build up a church too. It really is an incredibly inspiring story and is called *'A Life of Two Halves'*, a phrase which I seem to have heard somewhere before!

I feel constrained at this point not to move on, but to delve a little deeper in to my own fears that led me to ultimately put my life in the hands of another, Jesus, in my walk of faith.

A lot of money is being spent by Governments across the world to combat the threat of terrorism. Death is one terrorist, however, we will all have to come face to face with one day so it amazes me how little time is given to looking at this subject and seeing how we can combat this terrorist. I have been on two pre-retirement courses and incredibly, to my mind, death was not mentioned once. It was all about how to live life to the full, how to invest your money and so on. I believe it is vitally important that we prepare properly to die one day and that we examine all of the options rather than burying our heads in the sand.

In my book *Fear, Fun and Faith,* I outlined a number of my fears and how, one by one, I was able to overcome them. Strangely, even as a child the subject of death frightened me. One of my fascinations growing up was collecting caterpillars. I think the most I ever had at one time was four, but I would collect the jam jars, put some grass and leaves in and cover the top with a piece of paper and an elastic band to keep it in place. I would bodge holes in the top so the caterpillar could breathe. I tended them lovingly and caringly for a month or two and then felt really sad when they died and turned into a chrysalis. It was remarkable to see the caterpillar climb to the top of the jar and attach itself upside down to the lid. I kept a close eye on that apparently lifeless shell until a crack appeared. I would then gently turn the lid upside down and wait for an amazingly colourful butterfly to emerge and fly free from its shell. I was not often there when the butterfly emerged, but when I was, in my own child-like way I was awe struck. Tying this experience in with stories I heard at Sunday school about Jesus rising from the dead and his tomb being empty, made me think, "I wonder if that's what happens to us when we die?"

Taking that thought on into adulthood, at the back of my mind was always the thought that there must be life after death. My visit to

Westminster Chapel that one and only time somehow caused it all to make sense for me and I found my faith in Jesus.

Since then I have read much and listened to loads of different arguments on the subject of faith and life after death. In the end though, I remain convinced that it is possible through a personal relationship with Jesus Christ, to know total forgiveness for all of the wrong things I have thought, said and done and receive the completely free gift of everlasting life. Just as with the butterfly, my new body will be free from the restraints of this life. I don't know a whole lot more other than I believe it is going to be just brilliant.

One phrase from the Bible says that we get paid wages for our wrongdoing and those wages are death, but the free gift from God is eternal life. Now the thing about a gift is that you have to receive it. Someone could give you £1,000, as has happened with me, but if I had not taken it and said "thank you very much," then it would not be mine. I simply said thank you to God and received the gift of forgiveness and eternal life through Jesus. This is how I have chosen to deal with the subject of death. For me, the actions of Jesus Christ taking my sins to the cross and then being raised from the dead has dealt with my death terrorist once and for all.

Now it is for each one of us in the human race to decide for themselves. How are you going to deal with your terrorist? You can ignore him of course, but he will get you one day. Some people say when we die that is the end and we just go back to being dust. If that is your view, I fully respect that, providing you have properly thought it through and have not just buried your head in the sand.

It may be that you follow another religion and if that is the case, providing you have thought through all of the issues, then I fully respect and honour you for that. For me though, I say in the words of the song written by the late Andre Crouch *'Jesus is the answer for the world today, above Him there's no other, Jesus is the way.'*

If this has left you worried and confused then simply pray these words in the quietness of your own heart or out loud.....

"Dear God, if you are there, will you please make yourself known to me. I feel a bit confused so I ask you to make yourself known to me in ways that I can understand. Amen."

God loves you so much, just as a father and mother love their children, so if He is there, I promise you, He will answer your prayer. You have nothing to lose and an eternity to gain.

Chapter 6 - Trials and triumphs

Meanwhile back at HMRC things quietened down for a while as I got on with my regular paid job of processing tax cases. The worldwide recession and resulting austerity measures in the UK had meant that very little opportunity was being given for staff to leave their desks and attend classroom-type training, therefore the majority of our learning was computer based. Out of the blue, however, I was given an opportunity to do something I had not done before.

I was asked if I would undertake a BT Broadcast, which involved me being interviewed over the phone for 10 minutes. This broadcast would then be made available for the next few weeks for managers to dial in to and have a listen. I was asked questions which were designed to draw me out and talk about my experiences of effective management and naturally I drew on my own story and the massive impact John Dolan had had in encouraging me a few years earlier.

Well for such a short talk, the response we received was pretty outstanding and everyone involved in the project hailed it as a great success. Below is just a small sample of the massive amount of positive feedback we received;

"I have just listened to the first BT Broadcast and have to say that I was surprised with the content. I suppose I was not really sure what to expect and found this particular story really interesting and enjoyable. To hear it from John's viewpoint was different and made me very interested in his story."
Gordon Hannah

"The broadcast was interesting, so much of what John said his manager had done was common sense but it's so easy to forget or be too busy to take the time. Clearly it's a pity this light bulb

moment didn't occur earlier in John's career, sometimes it's just a case of finding the right button to press."
Lorraine Keats-Marsh

"John's story was certainly inspirational and I was struck by two things; firstly I think a massive part in John's success is down to his character - his optimism, his enthusiasm and generally just his lust for life. People like him are a gift to manage. Secondly, it's interesting that he spoke about the influence of a senior manager."
Charlotte Scrivens

"I have just listened to the Motivation broadcast and I'm feeling really motivated! John's story is inspiring in itself - so much to happen from just a few small words of encouragement followed up by some action. The story is a real reminder for us to remember the power of encouragement and the need for managers to open doors for other people where we can."
Sheila Hosker

"I thought this was 10 minutes well spent. How many times have we dedicated a whole day on a training event to get the same point! This was a much more efficient and effective method of delivery. Hearing an individual talk about their experience will stay with me much longer. I also thought it was a bit of a reality check. In the current climate with so many pressures and demands on manager's time, it is all too easy to forget to be human. I intend sharing this experience with my team and possibly use it to seek some feedback from them on how well or otherwise they feel I motivate them."
Alison Esson

"A couple of years ago I was able to arrange for John to come and 'do his thing' at my office as part of a learning at work/motivation/ team building exercise. Fear, Fun and Faith went down a storm and he ran with it twice that day as it was so popular!"
Melanie Donohoe

"I've just managed to listen to John's broadcast and I am so glad I did. What an inspiring story John has. You can pick out the 'go getters' in a team easily but when you have people who have been doing the same job for years, I think sometimes its human nature to assume that is their skill set. I also think the interview makes you think about how little it can take to give someone real encouragement and enthusiasm."
Jan Smith

"John's message is an inspiring one. I've heard him before but it was a useful reminder to me of the power of encouragement."
Jane Howard

"I really found John's story encouraging. It just shows how feedback and taking a genuine interest in the work people do can unlock potential and improve confidence. John's story also demonstrates how recognition can completely change people's perceptions of their own abilities and ambition. Thank you for sharing this with us John!"
Angela Geraghty

"John's message really covered what all managers 'should' be able to easily do and that is encourage, motivate and importantly praise good work. After another busy day of emails and meetings I found it a strong reminder never to take your team members for granted and such a small investment of your time as a manager can make a significant difference to an individual. I also think it highlighted the importance to spend time getting to know individuals to identify their skills and interests. It would have been all too easy to let John carry on as a typist until his retirement but instead the potential was identified and with a little encouragement not only has the business gained significantly from tapping into John's true abilities, but they have also now got a highly motivated and happy jobholder. As they say sometimes it's the little things that can make a big difference and this applies across all grades."

Alan Robinson

"An inspirational, almost humbling interview. Great to hear someone tell their story with such passion."
Steve Jefferies

"I enjoyed listening to this broadcast and you can imagine that his enthusiasm when working in a team environment would be infectious. It just makes you realise what effect a little bit of encouragement can have on a person and spur them on to achieve their goals, or even branch out into a direction they wouldn't have considered before."
Karen Boltwood

"I listened to John's broadcast a couple of weeks ago and intentionally delayed posting my comments to see if the initial impact (which was wholly positive) had been maintained. I'm happy to report that the initial 'feel-good factor' remains and I certainly feel more positive about management as a result. None of us want to admit it in this modern 'PC' society, but it is all too easy to overlook the aspirations (not to mention, untapped talents) of, in particular, older members of our teams. I don't want to be ageist and I realise that this wasn't the main message of the broadcast - there was a much wider 'motivation' message. However, I do think the 'coasting towards retirement' attitude (I think John used the phrase stuck in a rut) is one that managers can reluctantly find themselves accepting, particularly given the highly pressurised management roles most of us have these days. If nothing else, the broadcast has reminded me that everyone in a team has potentially untapped talents and it is our job to unearth them! I think John's statement that: "no-one ever died from an overdose of encouragement" is one that will always stick with me!!"
Peter Rae

Everyone involved in this pilot scheme was absolutely astounded by the overwhelmingly positive response to this broadcast. Using the modern vernacular, I think 'gobsmacked' is the word and this in turn led to me being invited to share my story in greater detail at a whole range of management meetings and conferences. There were still occasional invitations to go and share the *Fear, Fun and Faith* message, but more and more people, particularly managers, wanted to hear of my journey out of the rut and how my coasting to retirement mentality turned into being a highly motivated individual in love with his work. My next career development opportunity was only just around the proverbial corner.

Derek Hughes came to speak to staff in our business stream. Derek, based in Cardiff had been appointed as Assistant Director and he came along to introduce himself, outline some of the challenges we faced as a business area going forward into the digital age and discuss the inevitable job cuts. Not an easy message to deliver or indeed to receive, but I was impressed by Derek's gentle and compassionate style. Never one to hold back on the encouragement mail, I contacted Derek to thank him for taking the time to attend our office and to convey his message with such heartfelt warmth. I also took the opportunity to tell him something of my story for his encouragement.

Derek responded with his own email of appreciation and said that he had just been appointed as Disability Champion, he also mentioned that he had a sister by the name of Carole, who had suffered from spina bifida for around 50 years. Derek said his Mum and Dad had been Carole's full time carers for all of those years and his email touched me so deeply that I committed to praying for Carole on a regular basis. I was so thrilled a couple of years later when Derek let me know that after all these years his beloved sister had found true love and happiness.

A short while afterwards Derek was in touch again to say he had received funding for a very exciting project. Initially he had wanted to roll out a series of workshops to managers in our business stream relating to Disability Awareness. Once he had put his ideas to our Chief Executive, Lin Homer, however, she had been so inspired by this that she felt it should be made available to all managers within HMRC.

Derek told me something of his plans and that he needed some role models to help head up the project. I agreed to be one of those role models and in a short space of time I was being filmed at my office as I responded to questions about my career and experiences of good and bad management. The DVD, when completed, would form an integral part of the workshops. Later I had the honour of being chosen to compere the launch event in Manchester in the presence of a number of other inspiring role models as well as several Senior Civil Servants. More about that later though.

As so often has been the case throughout my life, it was not all plain sailing. Sylvia and I travelled to London to attend the wedding of a close family friend. The trouble was that I was taken ill the night before and admitted to St Thomas' Hospital with severe stomach pain. I was found to have an infection in the gall bladder along with a mass of gall stones.

Sadly Sylvia never did get to wear the lovely outfit she had bought for the occasion, she did, however, enjoy the view of the Houses of Parliament and Big Ben from my hospital window and I have to say, all of the staff at St Thomas' did a wonderful job of caring for me. In fact they were so good, we sent off a very appreciative snail-mail letter to the Hospital Administrator commending his team for the excellent standard of care they gave to me in the 24 hours or so I was there.

I am glad to say I did eventually have the gall bladder removed by keyhole surgery back in Birmingham and I have had no trouble since, not in that area anyway.

One area of my health that has caused me difficulties over the years is my loss of hearing. As a blind person, you will appreciate that my hearing is very special to me. Sadly, however, in recent years I have experienced a number of severe colds, which have gone straight to my head and ears, and the last two in particular have left me profoundly deaf and needing to resort to wearing hearing aids. The aids are magnificent I have to say and have added greatly to my quality of life in terms of being able to join in conversations without frequently having to say "Pardon?". In addition it has been a relief to Sylvia and other members of the family not to have to endure the television and CD's being played at such a high volume. Indeed I am the one now saying, "Can you turn it down please?"

The artificial sounds take some getting used to though. It has certainly made navigating my way around familiar routes a lot more difficult, because things sound so different. In addition music sounds different too and not having the best voice in the world, it sounds even worse to me when I am trying to sing along, particularly in church. Being hard of hearing is certainly proving to be quite a challenge and never more so than when I went to speak at an event in Manchester as my report of the day, below, will illustrate.

I want to tell you about a triumph that took place in Manchester on Tuesday 25th March 2014 and I am not talking about City beating United 3-0 before 76,000 supporters at the theatre of dreams otherwise known as Old Trafford.

This triumph began in my heart on Monday 24th March when I made up my mind to honour a commitment I had made to speak at an annual event for about 60 tax professionals. I was billed as the inspirational speaker however as well as being blind I had recently been struck down suddenly with an illness that had left me profoundly deaf.

Being deaf was and still is quite frightening and to all intents and purposes the best place to be is tucked away safely in my own home being cared for by my lovely wife and family. All of the natural senses and sound advice cried out 'ring up and apologise for your absence'.

This simply was not an option for me having spoken at length about overcoming fear, won a national award for it and even written a book about it. I am also a role model for people with disabilities and a champion of Diversity so what better opportunity for us all to pull together to make this work?

So with determination, and a certain amount of trepidation, I made up my mind to honour my commitment and travel to Manchester, whilst at the same time making it clear to the organisers of the event that I would need a little extra support.

Well from the time I set off from home at 6.15am to the time I arrived back at around 8.30pm I received so much in the way of loving care that I felt deeply humbled. Let me highlight for you some examples and if I miss one or two, they are no less important to me.

<u>Timetable for Tuesday 25 March</u>

6.15am - Someone picked me up by car to take me to a men's prayer meeting, where a few of the guys prayed for me and the day that lay ahead of me.

7am - Taxi driver picked me up from the church to take me to my office in Birmingham.

7.30am - Arrived in the office where I received a kind and compassionate response from my manager when I explained just how deaf I am.

9am - A lady designated by my manager escorted me to New Street Station and she waited with me until a member of the station staff took me to my train and guided me to my seat.

9.50am - The train arrived in Wolverhampton where four of the people I was due to be speaking with met me and sat with me for much of the journey.

11am - Arrived in Manchester and was escorted with my colleagues to a taxi and then on to the Ramada Hotel for the final day of the two day annual team event.

11.30am - I was introduced to three or four other people who would take responsibility for me during the course of the day, including a man on toilet duty!

12.30pm - Went to lunch in the restaurant and once again I was served and waited on to a very high standard.

In the afternoon I sat through several hours of business sessions and that was the hardest for me because I could hardly hear a word that was said, just picking up bits and pieces here and there. When it came time for me to wind up the day with my talk I was introduced in a professional manner, placed in the right spot so that I was facing my audience and off I went.

I felt a warmth and a receptivity coming from my audience and the prolonged applause at the end seemed to indicate a lot of appreciation. I had done what I had set out to achieve in that I had honoured my commitment and by the grace of God I was able to bring some much needed encouragement and inspiration to folk who work in a high pressure environment.

My day of being loved and cared for was topped off in wonderful style. A lady who, herself, is a carer for her sick husband, came all the way to Birmingham with me and then saw me safely on to a taxi heading for home. She then caught the train back to Wolverhampton to get her connection for Telford.

I was astounded by the success of the day, despite my own circumstances. I felt so vulnerable for much of the time, but all the while was surrounded by so many people who love, care and go the extra mile. This was truly a day when we saw disability awareness and diversity come to the fore - a day of triumph indeed.

It was only a week later and I was back in Manchester again, this time to compete the aforementioned Disability launch event. My ears had still been bad, but a wonderful thing happened in church on the morning before I was due to travel. During the worship time as the band played and I tried hard to join in with the singing, both of my ears popped.

I was so amazed, even excited, I exclaimed "I can hear". Sylvia enquired as to what had happened and I told her in a much quieter tone, but it was such a relief.

I was able to attend the launch event and though my hearing was far from perfect, I could hear enough of each speaker so as to link each item together with an appropriate comment. I had a lovely surprise at the end of the day in that each of the role models were presented with a Pacesetter Industry Award for being inspiring role models for people with disabilities. The framed certificate was presented to each one of us by Mark Dearnley, Chief Digital Officer and Disability Champion for HMRC.

Chapter 7 - A way with words

Earlier, when talking about church, I alluded to the fact that I enjoy attending live events as opposed to being an 'armchair' type. Ever since I was a child of about 8 years of age I guess, I have loved the magic of the cinema. My parents were not ones for attending the cinema, or 'the pictures' as we called them in those days, so I could not wait until I was old enough to go by myself or with my mates. One of the first films I can recall seeing was called Pal Joey and starred Frank Sinatra, but I cannot recall anything of the story line. Personally I really enjoyed the westerns both on the big screen and on the television. I also liked the comedies and I became a massive fan of the Carry On films starting right back with the first one *Carry on Sergeant* which was a spin-off from the television series *The Army Game.*

When Sylvia and I first met we found it most romantic going out to the pictures together. We used to have to try and find a quiet spot in the cinema because Sylvia was constantly whispering into my ear; not so much words of affection, but she was describing what was happening on the screen for me. I found it particularly exciting at one point, while we were still dating (I have avoided the old fashioned word courting, because I never did like that one!) when one of our favourite cinemas introduced a late night double bill on a Friday night. I had to get permission from Sylvia's Dad to keep her out late. I used to like the *Hammer House of Horrors* and the first double bill we saw, through squinted eyes, or ears in my case, was *The Pit and the Pendulum* and *Drops of blood*, both of which I think starred the great actor Vincent Price. Why, even his voice was creepy! Come to think of it, it's a wonder Sylvia married me after that isn't it? She may well have thought, "What kind of a nutter am I going out with anyway?"

I say all of this by way of a backdrop to suggest that once in a while you get a movie that makes a deep impact on you. *Mandela: The Long Walk to Freedom* was such a movie for me. Bearing in mind I could not see the visuals and just had the audio track to go by, the impact on me was mesmerising and life-changing. At the end of the film I sat in my seat for several minutes shaking and with tears streaming from my eyes. Something had happened in my heart as I listened to this incredible man's life story being played out on the big screen.

I think the main thing that hit me was this; never again could I say to myself "I am only one person, so what difference can I make?

Down through history there have been hundreds, even thousands of individuals who have been used to bring transformation to their nation and indeed to the world. The simple truth is if you have a burning passion and a dream that nothing can dampen, then there is absolutely nothing you cannot achieve. The key is to have the dream and the passion. Nelson Mandela had a dream that all people are equal regardless of race, colour, education etcetera and his passion was that there would come a time in South Africa when every person would have an equal say in how their country was run.

Through more than a quarter of a century of discouragement, torture and outright humiliation, Mandela did not let his dream and love for people die. Even when it would have been easier to hate, he chose the way of love and at the God-appointed time, he won the day. The life of Nelson Mandela, though far from perfect, impacted not only on South Africa, but many parts of the world as well.

So how was this relevant to me? Rightly or wrongly I connected this to my work situation and the awesome opportunities that were coming my way, where I was given the immense privilege of being able to speak into people's lives via my presentations. Within my heart there is a really deep joy and appreciation of this precious gift of life and I want to give that away to my audiences. If it's true what Dr Chan Abraham said, that a great many people in the UK are living a Monday to Friday death, then there is a lot of negativity I can speak into and seek to change by planting a seed in people's work life mentality.

Of course it's one thing to theorise, but it's totally different when it comes to doing something about it. I began to dream and pray about making HMRC a wonderful place in which to work, but I had to start where I was in Birmingham. It was all about making sure my attitude was right. I made a point of saying "Good morning" on arriving at work and that started with our security guards at the front of our building. One day, Ray, one of the guards said in response to my cheery "Good morning", "What's good about it? It's Monday morning and peeing down with rain".

I replied by saying, "Well Ray, you are alive aren't you? You could be dead and you're a long time dead, now that's something to be grateful for so cheer up, because life isn't all bad".

After that he always made a point of saying "Good morning" and putting the emphasis on the good. Interesting that because have you noticed nowadays, if people do speak in the morning, they often just say "Morning"? What does that mean and where did the good go? Similarly people say "Love you". I often respond, "Who loves me?" I believe the words we speak are powerful and it is important not to leave the good off in "Good Morning" or the I in "I love you". I must stress the seriousness in the language we use and the way in which we say it. Our words are important, they are powerful and they have the ability to either create or destroy.

On my team one day, a lady came back from the kitchen and related an incident to me saying that another woman had taken offence at something she had said. My colleague followed up by asking "Would you be offended at that?"

My reply was to say "I made up my mind years ago not to be offended".

She was rather taken aback by this response and has often referred to it since, thinking it to be pretty amazing. I have learned over the years that we do have the ability to make quality decisions which affect the way we live and the way we treat others. If I take offence then the person being most at risk will be me because I give place to resentment, bitterness and hatred, which ultimately work like a cancer within me and I do not want that. I have made a choice to walk in love, forgiveness and mercy. I don't always succeed, but I find that when I am out of sync as it were my conscience, or is it God, will let me know and I have the opportunity to put it right. I firmly believe it is possible to change if we have a mind to do so. I used to be one of those people who would say "I am not a morning person". I would often say that kind of thing to excuse my grumpiness at the start of a day.

This was never truer than when our three daughters were very young and they would wake up at about 7am full of life and energy. Of course they would bound into Mum and Dad's bedroom expecting us to be equally bright and cheerful. The opposite was true, however, as I closed my eyes and pretended to still be sleeping, although in the end though I would have to admit defeat and get up to face the day in a rather begrudging way. I did not like my attitude one little bit and I felt guilty for being so irritable.

It was time to change and that demanded some radical action. I told Sylvia I was going to set the alarm clock for 6am. I actually put the clock on the other side of the bedroom so I had to get out of bed quickly so it did not wake up everyone else in the house. On getting up I was able to quietly wash, make a cup of tea downstairs and then have a short time of prayer, thanking God for the night, the new day and all that lay ahead. When the children did eventually come bounding down the stairs they found Daddy in a much happier frame of mind. I was then able to take Sylvia a cup of tea and she was able to arise to a house which had a much more pleasant atmosphere. Now all these years later, I love early mornings. They are my favourite part of the day, at least for feeling bright, alert and energetic. I am a morning person, because I have trained myself to be.

Generosity is another one of my favourite subjects. I love to be generous with my words, attitudes and actions. When I go to work I want to be fully present and give my whole self to it. It is so easy to attend work, but not actually be present. If, in your heart, you really don't want to be at work, then I would ask, "Are you fully present?" In any activity or relationship and that goes for work too, the more we commit ourselves to it, the more we can expect to receive back. If I am generous with my words and actions then somehow things have a habit of coming back to you in a positive way.

A few years ago I, along with three or four colleagues, decided to form an office-based Christian Fellowship. The idea was that we would come together for half an hour each week on a lunchtime to pray for one another and for our colleagues. Over the years our numbers, at least on our circulation list, have grown to around the 40 mark, though an average of around 10 people actually get to meet each week. During this time we have been able to support many colleagues through tough times, letting them know we are praying for them, sending them cards, flowers and other words of encouragement.

In the last couple of years we decided to take this to a whole new level. We wanted to extend generosity and unconditional love to our work colleagues so at Easter we bought 1,000 Easter eggs to give away, whilst at Christmas we purchased the same number of mince pies. It's just about creating a different atmosphere and generating a sense of family and friendliness in an often stressful business environment. We are just doing what we can to make the workplace, where after all, is where most of us spend the majority of our time, a much happier place to be.

I would also point out that in our building there is a great deal of other good work going on as well in terms of people of other faiths and no faith at all performing some amazing acts of charity and kindness. *Children In Need* is always really well supported and various charities throughout the year benefit from sales of samosas (always the most popular!), books, DVD's as well as home-made cakes and crafts. I absolutely love going out to work and I am going to miss it big time when I retire, sorry re-fire, shortly.

In truth, leaving HMRC in 2015 was not at all part of my plan. Indeed I was rather chuffed, to put it mildly, that after nearly 30 years working in the Civil Service I had just earned my first promotion. I had been offered the chance to move to Solihull, near where I live, as part of HMRC Special Investigations working at Administrative Officer (AO) level, which is one step up from the

Administrative Assistant (AA) grade that I had been on for my entire career.

I was due to visit the new office and meet up with my prospective manager to discuss the job and test it out for accessibility purposes. About a week before this was due to take place, however, the Department announced that they were introducing a Voluntary Exit Scheme for people in the AA grade within our business stream. With the onset of digitalisation, there was clearly a need to reduce the number of people working at AA level. Having agreed to accept promotion I thought I had just missed out on this, but was pleasantly surprised to find that as I had not yet officially taken up my new duties, I was still eligible to apply for the Voluntary Exit Scheme. Thus, I declined my promotion and applied for my release under the exit scheme. My request was granted and so at the age of 68 I will be walking away from HMRC with an unexpected but most welcome golden handshake. This will enable me to invest a little bit of money into launching my new business, but more of that later.

Chapter 8 - A tale of two palaces

My incredible story has now almost come full circle. We started at Bitzaro Palace and very soon now, we will be heading off to Buckingham Palace to receive my MBE. Firstly, however, I want to say how very grateful I am to my management team in City Centre House, Birmingham for taking the time and trouble to nominate me for this honour. I understand the process of doing that is not an easy one and it is pretty time-consuming in terms of gathering evidence. I only discovered fairly recently that much of the work for this was done by the aforementioned John Dolan, the very man who 10 years ago saw something in me to the point where he was willing to invest in my personal development.

This is so poignant for the following reason. Early in 2014 I received an email from John, who was then working in Cardiff as part of Criminal Investigations. He said that after 40 years in the Department, he had decided to retire so he could spend more time with his family and build his dream house. Shortly afterwards I went off on a couple of weeks annual leave, spent in Weston-Super-Mare with Sylvia. On my return to the office I was absolutely devastated to discover an email from one of John's colleagues to say that just a few weeks into his retirement he had suffered a massive heart attack and died, at the age of 57.

I could not believe it and the grief I felt was akin to losing a close family member. I wrote to John's widow Jane and his two grown up children to express my sorrow and deep sympathy for them, but my words felt hollow. To her immense credit I did receive a most touching letter from Jane a little while later. To think though, that the man who had done so much for me and then nominated me for an honour from the Queen did not live to see the outcome of his work.

I have campaigned recently to see whether in John's honour we can introduce within HMRC, or even the wider Civil Service, an annual award. This would give staff the opportunity to vote for any manager they felt worthy to receive *'The Inspirational Line Manager of the Year Award'*. This would be an incentive for managers to be proactive in developing their staff and would also give team members a practical way of thanking managers who had truly helped them develop and realise their potential. Such an award would also, in time, be a source of comfort to John's family, if they knew that his legacy was living on in such a positive way.

Just before publication of this book I have heard from the Cabinet Office that my recommendation has been taken up. This year 2015 will be the 10th year of the Civil Service Awards and to celebrate the fact it will be held at Buckingham Palace in November. I have been invited along as a guest together with John's widow Jane. I am so thrilled about this

The Investiture

It's been a long wait, but the day finally arrived for us to depart to London. I went into work this morning and left at 11am, caught my regular taxi home with Sarfraz and in about 30 minutes I walked into the house. I was greeted by Allison, who asked how I was feeling. I told her I felt strangely nervous, but felt sure the butterflies in the stomach would soon pass. I quickly changed into a fresh set of casual clothes, sorted out my overnight case with Allison's assistance and before too long Sylvia and I were waiting for our friends Paul and Carole to arrive.

In no time at all, the four of us were heading off in Paul's car to Birmingham International railway station to catch the Virgin train to London Euston. Paul had managed to get a great deal for the outward journey to London - four first class tickets at £16 each - it was a different story for the homeward journey, however, but never mind. Regardless of that we enjoyed our bargain as we sat in comfortable, spacious seats and were served no end of drinks, exotic sandwiches, cakes and other nibbles. What a lovely way it was to start this memorable occasion.

Because we had booked 'Passenger Assistance', when we arrived at Euston we were greeted by a very friendly guy who transported us from the train to the waiting taxis, and in no time at all we were heading for our overnight destination, the Thistle Hotel.

The hotel staff were great and could not do enough for us. We were shown to our room on the second floor. Sylvia and I were in room 201 and Paul and Carole were in an adjoining room number 202. For Sylvia, this had been the longest she had stayed awake for many months and she was more than grateful to be able to throw herself on to the bed for a much-needed rest, after unpacking the case of course and setting up my CPAP machine.

For the uninitiated those letters stand for Continuous Positive Air Pressure. You see, I have suffered from sleep apnoea for more than 10 years now. After years of heavy snoring, I went to see a Doctor when I was concerned about my extreme levels of tiredness, including falling asleep at my office computer and short bouts of memory loss. The perceptive Doctor asked if I snored and if my wife ever said I stopped breathing. I said that she did fear that and also when I awoke I gave a loud snort. I was referred to a sleep clinic and I had to wear a small contraption one night around my finger and during my sleep this measured a number of things including my breathing, heart rate etc. The results revealed that I was stopping breathing for over 200 times a night for anything up to 10 to 15 seconds at a time, making me a high risk for a stroke due to the lack of oxygen to the brain. This went some way to explaining my extreme tiredness and impaired memory functions.

So it was I was prescribed a CPAP machine which means I have to wear a mask whenever I go to sleep at night. To begin with I found this quite distressing and so did Sylvia; she wondered quite who, or what, she was going to bed with and one night I remember we cried together about it. Jokingly, I did try to lighten the mood by saying "One night in a fit of passion you could try and unmask me".

Uncomfortable as it was, the positive thing was that I stopped snoring, felt more refreshed and my memory improved. We have had to take that machine everywhere with us and that includes holidays, overnight stays and into hospital on the odd occasion I have needed treatment. Happily over the years, the machines have decreased in size and the masks are ever so slowly becoming a little more comfortable. After a short rest in our hotel room, it was time to have a wash and freshen up in time for our evening meal. We went to the hotel dining room, where we enjoyed a fabulous meal and had some friendly banter with the Portuguese, Spanish and Lithuanian waiters and waitresses.

I think Paul and Carole retired to watch a little television, but Sylvia and I headed straight to bed, or almost. Sylvia did try having a bath but she could not get the water to run hot. In the end having stood there naked and shivering for a few minutes she decided to give up and go to bed. I decided to go and give the taps another try and initially managed to get soaked as I turned on the shower by mistake. After a little more persistence I did manage to work out how the taps worked and I enjoyed a somewhat hotter than usual bath.

Before going to sleep Sylvia and I held hands in bed as we had done for many months since her stroke, thanked God for a good day and looked forward in faith to what Friday 13th February 2015 held in store for us.

On Friday 13th June 2014 we had set off for our holiday at Bitzaro Palace and now some eight months later, on Friday 13th February 2015 we were heading for Buckingham Palace. We could not have planned it more perfectly had we tried, but no doubt in our minds, whatsoever, God was in this.

After a hearty breakfast (full English for me of course!) We went back to our rooms to change into our very best apparel. Sylvia and I had enjoyed going shopping for new clothes as had all of our four grown up kids. The colour scheme was most definitely blue, although it did not reflect our mood. I have to say I am not totally at home in a suit, referring more the smart casual option. This was a rather special once in a lifetime opportunity to look our very best and I am reliably informed that Sylvia looked especially stunning, as did our three daughters. As for Ian and me, well I think we looked okay too!

At the Investiture we were allowed four tickets in all, i.e. myself and three guests. There was no way we could choose from two of our four children and that is why we invited our close friends Paul and Carole. Beverley, Sara, Allison and Ian would join us outside of Buckingham Palace afterwards for photographs and then on for a meal. At 9am we were greeted by Jason who was driving a big, blacked out Mercedes, as Paul had arranged through a business colleague for us to be chauffeur-driven to and from the Palace. This was certainly a case of 'doing it in style'.

As we wended our way slowly (is there any other way?) through the London streets, my fellow passengers enjoyed spotting the familiar landmarks like Trafalgar Square, Westminster Abbey, Big Ben and so on as well as the famous shopping districts in the case of the ladies. Even at that stage, I have to admit wondering to myself, just how tired Sylvia might be feeling. I just hoped and prayed adrenaline would carry her through the day.

Soon we were approaching Buckingham Palace and it was Paul who broke the news. The Union Jack was flying at the Palace which meant that the Queen was not in residence. I certainly did not know that bit of Royal trivia and I have to admit to feeling a little sense of disappointment. Queen Elizabeth II has in my opinion given truly outstanding service to our country and it would have been an incredible honour and privilege to meet her in person. Had it have been the Duke of Cambridge conducting the Investiture, I had joked that I would chat with him about the sad plight of Aston Villa, of whom I believe, he is a supporter.

On driving into the Palace grounds we went through several strict security checks on the vehicle as well as on us, checking Passports etc. Once actually inside, the Palace staff were on hand at almost every corner to offer assistance and give guidance. Sylvia, who we had taken in a wheelchair, was allowed to go upstairs on the lift, accompanied by a member of staff. Paul, Carole and I took the opportunity to walk up the staircases and that was an education in itself. There was no particular smell that I could describe, but the carpets were plush and there were a great many paintings, mostly large ones, covering different periods of history and from a range of countries. There were also a good many statues, even nude ones, so I was told.

Eventually when we were reunited with Sylvia, it was explained to us that Sylvia could go with Carole and take their places in the ballroom, whilst Paul could accompany me with the other people receiving awards into another room, where the protocol would be explained to us.

On the day there were about 100 people receiving awards from all walks of life, including the Armed Forces and the Police. We were offered a glass of apple juice or water while we waited around chatting to one another. It will not test your powers of intuition too much to guess what the most asked question was that was doing the rounds - "What have you received your award for?"

The people Paul and I spoke with mainly had been recognised for their charity work, though we did also speak with a local Councillor and a member of the Royal Air Force.

It was a Colonel, we later discover who came and explained what would happen during the ceremony and to tell us it was the Her Royal Highness, the Princess Royal who would be performing the Investiture. The main thing to remember was that we were to say "Good morning Your Royal Highness", and in the men's case just give a bow of the head as a mark of respect. Princess Anne would then lean forward and pin on the medal before engaging each person in a short conversation. At its conclusion, the Princess would shake you by the hand and that was the signal to step back and turn away, having first of all said "Thank you Mam".

Having arrived at the Palace at about 10am the ceremony began at 11am prompt. People were called through in groups of about 12 at a time and taken along a corridor to wait at the entrance of the ballroom until your name was announced. As we waited our turn, there was a large screen showing events in the ballroom and just before the Investiture began the cameras panned around the room and Paul was able to tell me that Sylvia (in her wheelchair) and Carole were sat right on the front row with an amazing view of proceedings. It was clear too that a light orchestra was also playing. The National anthem was played as the ceremony began and the first recipients began to file forward.

As Paul and I sat and observed, I was introduced to Clare, a member of staff, who told me that she had been designated to walk me the last few steps up to Princess Anne and then lead me safely back to Paul afterwards. Clare, possibly sensing I was a little nervous, reassured me that all would be fine. I had rehearsed the line "Good morning Your Majesty" for so many months, I was now afraid of saying that to the Princess Royal, instead of "Your Royal Highness".

Slowly but surely the names were being called, but clearly on this particular day we were going to have to be patient. I was in the last group to be called and with Clare alongside Paul and me we made our way towards the ballroom.

Having ascertained we would have about a 15 minute wait in the line before my turn came, I decided to engage Clare in some conversation. I was interested to know more about her job, how long she had worked at the Palace and so on.

Clare said she had been born in Bolton and spent much of her early life in Blackpool. I think she said her background had been in the hospitality industry and just for a bit of a laugh she decided to look on the Buckingham Palace website to see what jobs were going. She came across a vacancy for someone within her field of experience so she decided to apply, never thinking for one minute, she would be called for an interview. The call did come, however and the rigorous interview lasted around eight hours. Clare said she could not believe it when the letter came, offering her the position. The official title she has is 'Page of the Presence' which she said is a really ancient position, which basically does what it says, i.e. ushers people into the presence of Royalty. Clare clearly loves her job and gets to go out on visits with the Queen. For what it is worth, Clare also asked about me and the work I do. I told her I was writing this book and promised to send her a copy when it was published.

The conversation came to an abrupt end when Clare said "It's your turn next. Are you okay?"

I said I was and then I heard the announcer saying "Mr John Flanner, awarded an MBE for services to Her Majesty's Revenue and Customs".

I walked forward with Clare at my side and I knew once she tapped my arm and let go that I must be in front of the Princess Royal, so I said "Good morning Your Royal Highness".

With that the Princess leaned forward and pinned the medal on my suit jacket.

"Congratulations," she said, "how long have you worked for the Inland Revenue?"

"Nearly 30 years" I replied.

"Were you already blind when you started there?" she queried.

I responded, "Yes, I started as an audio typist, but then about 11 years ago things changed and I began to give talks at team meetings in order to try and improve morale and raise awareness of diversity issues".

To be truthful I was on a roll at this point, so Princess Anne politely interjected as only someone with vast experience can do, "Well again many congratulations, you have no doubt inspired lots of people".

With that she took my right hand and shook it. I knew this was my cue to close the conversation so I stepped back a couple of paces, bowed my head at least once, maybe more and said "Thank you Mam".

Clare was then at my side to deliver me safely back into Paul's care. At that point another member of the Palace staff congratulated me and removed my medal so he could put it into a very nice presentation box. Paul and I were then guided to the back of the ballroom where we sat and waited for the last few people to receive their awards. It was only then, once I could totally relax, that I could appreciate the sweet, gentle music of the orchestra.

When the final recipient had received his award, for services in Afghanistan, we all stood for the National Anthem and then the Princess Royal was escorted from the ballroom. After a respectful few seconds of silence, people then began to leave in a gentle fashion. Clare came over and told us we would get to meet up with Sylvia again at the bottom of the stairs by the lift. It felt like a pretty long wait, but ultimately Sylvia did come through with Carole and we made our way out of the Palace and back to the waiting Mercedes and our lovely driver Jason.

It was noticeable how in the three hours we had been inside the Palace the temperature had dropped considerably and with the rain beginning to fall it felt pretty bitter. As we drove towards the exit gate, Paul was able to make contact with our son Ian by phone and from that we deduced that our kids were waiting outside. It was great to meet them and give them a hug. They had only been waiting around for about 10 minutes, but they were all cold and wet. Thankfully, the ever-dependable Jason had got several Mercedes umbrellas in the car so we were all able to make use of them. We all posed for photographs, trying hard not to look quite as cold and shivering as we were, and the hope is that at least one of them would be good enough for the front cover of this book. Time will tell.

Dave Edwards, a graphic designer friend from Renewal and his wife Rachel, who is editing this story, travelled down to London to take the professional photographs and as it fell on St Valentine's weekend, decided to stay over in London for a spot of sightseeing.

We headed off to Brunswick Square for a meal at Carluccios, which I have to say, was pretty sensational, we all loved it. Sylvia who was looking extremely fatigued by this time, revitalised noticeably at her first taste of calamari! We had lots of banter as we reminisced about the day. Unfortunately for the second time within a few hours I managed to splash something down my tie and one member of our party, who shall be nameless, said the MBE stood for "messy bloody eater" and who was I to argue in light of the evidence.

With the rain still bucketing down, it was time to call the taxis and make our way back to Euston station. Booked on to the crowded 5pm virgin train we arrived back into Birmingham International at about 6.20pm and once Paul had collected his car, we were heading home and back in the house by 6.45pm. Sylvia wasted no time at all in heading for a hot bath and getting into bed feeling pretty exhausted. I was dashing around doing a few little odd jobs and still wearing my suit and brand new shoes, I managed to slip down the stairs banging my arms and giving myself a bloody nose.

I suppose that is one way to keep an MBE's feet very firmly on the ground, along of course with splashing things down one's tie!

On reflection this had been an unforgettable occasion for us as a family and for our dear friends Paul and Carole, who I have to say, really did care for Sylvia and me impeccably. I have much to say in praise of the staff at Buckingham Palace in terms of their kindness and professionalism. I would like to make one critical observation though. Apart from a small glass of water or apple juice we were offered nothing else by way of refreshment. Even worse to my way of thinking, our guests, who were at the Palace for three hours in total received not so much as a glass of water.

Now let me ask you this question, if someone came to visit your house, would you leave them even as much as one hour, without offering them a drink? If it was simply up to Her Majesty the Queen I am sure she would be much more hospitable. I am confident it is not a matter of finance, so is it a logistical issue? I feel confident a Royal House that is as efficiently run as Buckingham Palace would have no trouble in arranging soft drinks and a few nibbles for around 400 guests, for whom this day is more often than not, a once in a lifetime experience.

As I often say, "You never get a second chance to make a first impression". Having made that point though, this will not detract from what was a truly memorable day and one which will live in the memory for the rest of our lives.

Chapter 9 - Retired and refired!

Here we are then; it's Wednesday 1st April 2015, 47 days on from our trip to Buckingham Palace and this is my first day of retirement. It's hard to believe I have actually walked out of City Centre House in Birmingham for the very last time as an HMRC employee.

Since departing the gates of Buckingham Palace with my MBE safely tucked away in its commemorative box, I have had an interesting few weeks to say the least. You could say it has been a fairly typical representation of my life to date, with some highs and some lows, but certainly NEVER BORING. Here are the highlights:

Fascinating Aida

A few days after the exciting day at Buckingham Palace we had a belated Christmas present to look forward to. Ian and Gemma (his lovely wife) had decided to treat us all (Sylvia, myself and our three daughters) to a trip to the Lichfield Garrick Theatre to attend a concert by *Fascinating Aida*. This is not a touring opera company but a trio of fairly posh sounding ladies performing a range of self-penned satirical and occasionally irreverent songs, with piano accompaniment. Adele, Dillie and Liza, to give *Fascinating Aida* their individual names, first came to our attention when our daughter Beverley played us their song called *Cheap Flights* on YouTube. It was hilarious and we loved it. A further Google search led us to discover the brilliant *Tesco Saves* which is sung in the style of a black Gospel Church

This night out was to be Sylvia's first since her stroke well over six months earlier. It was going to be quite a challenge for her because she still gets very fatigued and likes to be in bed by around 7pm. Anyway travelling the 40 minutes or so by car to Lichfield was tough for Sylvia and she held on in the back for grim life. Once we arrived at the small, but very engaging theatre, we made our way to our seats and at least for the first half of the show, Sylvia really enjoyed it, along with the rest of us. At the interval though, Sylvia put her coat on and when we asked what she was doing, she said she was going home. She genuinely thought it was the end, or hoped it was. It was not that the concert was bad, far from it in fact, Sylvia was just very worn out and wanted her bed.

We did get through until almost the end and we arrived home close to 11pm. Needless to say, Sylvia made her way quickly to bed, leaving Ian to reflect that maybe it wasn't the best Christmas present he had ever purchased. *Fascinating Aida* themselves were excellent in concert though and providing you have a reasonably broad mind, then I would recommend them for a really funny evening of entertainment. A song that we had not heard before, but a real favourite of ours from the show is called *Boomerang Kids*. If you give it a listen then many modern day parents will be able to relate to the clever lyrics in this song.

Premier Radio interview

As with many blind people, radio has been a close companion of mine over the years. It is a bit of a standing joke in our family in fact and Sylvia has often said that I am going to be buried (or was it cremated?) with all of my radios, because there is never one far from my side. Now with the advent of DAB, I have more radios than ever and I passionately explain that each one has a reason for

113

being in our house. I still don't think the family are convinced though.

For about 15 years I helped out on what was Radio Birmingham, now BBC WM. To begin with I would review my favourite Country Gospel records on a show called Country Style, presented by Ken Dudeny. When that show finished I was moved on to a Sunday morning slot to review the latest Christian music releases in a programme called *A Word in Advance*, which for many years was presented by Reverend Michael Blood, a great name for a Vicar I thought! When I moved to the South West for a while later in life I also helped out with programmes on BBC Radio Devon and Cornwall.

To be honest I would have loved to have had the opportunity to present my own music show on radio. I adore music and I enjoy choosing songs that contain a message in the lyrics. From my own experience I feel that God has often spoken to me through a song, let alone the incredible memories music evokes. The letters we received at the radio stations too also indicated just how powerful music is when it comes to stirring the emotions, bringing comfort and inspiration. Those are the reasons why I would relish the role of presenting a radio music show, where I had influence in choosing the music.

All that is by way of introduction to say that I received an invitation to be a guest on the breakfast show on *Premier Radio* in London in February 2015. The programme was hosted by John Pantry, who was well known to me in my earlier Christian life as he was a touring singer-songwriter, probably best known for his brilliant song called *Empty-handed*.

At first I thought I would have to travel to London and stay overnight at a Premier Inn near the studios in Pimlico. That thought did not thrill me though as it would mean another night away from Sylvia. As I was mulling over my options, I remember something a man from church had said a few weeks before.

Graham said, "If you ever need help of any kind, such as a lift to church, then do not hesitate to give me a ring".

The offer seemed very genuine so I gave Graham a quick phone call, explained the scenario and left it with him. In a short while he rang me back to say he would take me to London on the early morning train and get me to the studios. Graham, a retired solicitor (yet now busier than ever!), sorted everything out, including booking and paying for the tickets.

That morning my alarm was set for 4.15am and Graham arrived at my house in good time for us to catch the train to London Euston. We chatted all the way, getting to know each other a lot better. Once in London, a quick trip on the tube saw us in no time at all at the studios of *Premier Radio*. We were greeted by the lovely Lisa, who quickly arranged for the obligatory, refreshing cup of tea.

I was called into the studio while the 8am news was being broadcast, introduced to John Pantry and given a basic run down of the format for the following 50 minutes or so. John interviewed me about my work within HMRC, what it was like to go blind, how I became a Christian and what it was like going in to receive my MBE. I was able to mention that I was also setting up my own business, but more on that shortly. I thoroughly enjoyed being back behind the microphone, although I was sorry to cause John to run slightly overtime and into the news – a cardinal sin for a professional broadcaster – unless it *BBC Radio 5 Live* of course, because they do it all the time.

Broadcasting on radio always throws up its fair share of surprises and this was no exception. No sooner had I left the studio than a phone call came through for me and it was from a dear friend by the name of Gerald Heasley, a pal of ours from over 35 years ago. Gerald had been a Pastor at the Church of the Nazarene (I love that name!) in Northfield, Birmingham. Now after all these years we are back in touch and avidly swapping emails.

I received about two dozen other emails, many of which were very moving stories, and all saying how the interview had been a source of encouragement, comfort and inspiration. If you should want to watch it then you can do a Google search, type in 'blind man leads the sighted' on *YouTube* and hopefully you will find me there.

Cancer scare

Health challenges seem to be never far from our door and yet again we have experienced a bit of a fright. Before and after the Palace visit I had been experiencing some pretty unpleasant symptoms with bowels and water works culminating in me having to take a series of antibiotics to try and clear up any lingering infection. I had also had a couple of questionable blood test results; one showing that my red blood cell count was down and the other that my PSA (prostate specific antigen) level had shot up pretty dramatically. An appointment was made for me to see Mr Phillips, the urologist at Solihull Hospital and he wasted no time in telling me that there was a one in three chance I had got prostate cancer and arranged for me to have a biopsy at Heartlands Hospital.

My daughter Allison, left Sylvia in someone else's care, while she accompanied me to the hospital. In the waiting area there were six of us nervous-looking men awaiting the procedure. Allison and one or two other ladies who were accompanying their men folk, engaged in some humorous banter to try and bring a smile or two. Questions like "Has anyone had this done before?" and "Is it very painful?" were doing the rounds as we all tried to put on a brave face.

I have to say that supported, as I was, by a lot of people praying for me, I did feel pretty relaxed. The nursing staff helped a lot because they were friendly and extremely understanding as one by one we were called to be weighed, measured for height and required to do a urine sample. Another really compassionate, caring nurse then explained the procedure and said she would give us two suppositories; one was an antibiotic and the other was a painkiller. Once these had been inserted I was then asked to go and sit back in the waiting room, until it was time for my biopsy to take place. By this time Allison had been and fetched me a very welcome cup of tea from the refreshment area and I downed it with much relish.

Whilst drinking my tea, a couple of the men had already been in for their procedure and came out not sounding too bad at all which significantly helped to raise the courage levels. No sooner had I finished the last dregs of my cup than it was my turn. A different, but still friendly nurse guided me into the room, where I was led to a bed. By this time of course I was wearing one of those most immodest hospital gowns. I was told to lie on the bed on my left side in the recovery position. A male doctor then came over and asked me to raise my legs up a little and he told me he was going to insert a probe into my back passage and whilst it would not hurt it may feel slightly uncomfortable. That done (and yes it was!) he explained that they were going to take 14 biopsies from different

117

parts of my prostate and that each one might be a little sharp and that I would hear a clicking sound as each one was taken. About half of them were just like having a normal injection, but the other half I hardly felt a thing.

Within five minutes or so, it was all over and a very kind nurse brought me an even better cup of tea than I had received previously, for this one was actually in a proper mug, and it tasted great. Once I was dressed and ready to leave, I was given three days' worth of antibiotics and instructed to return to the outpatients' clinic two weeks later for the results.

As with a lot of these medical tests there is very little really to be afraid of, even for us men, but it is the waiting game that is often the most difficult. It is in those times that the mind can really play tricks with you. I can only reiterate that when lots of people are praying for you then you feel so strengthened and so much more at peace than you could ever imagine. It was like that for me when Sylvia was so desperately ill in Zante and once again I experienced it at this time while I was awaiting the results of the biopsy.

My outpatient's appointment was on the same morning and at the same time as the partial solar eclipse and on the way to the hospital the taxi driver kept stopping to take a look at the sun and the moon. He was awe-struck at the sights he saw and Allison was busy taking photographs with her phone from the back of the taxi. When we arrived at Heartlands Hospital we were faced by a string of medical people outside looking up at the sky and taking their own photographs on an array of mobile devices.

Anyway once inside the waiting area I was greeted by a Japanese guy who was one of the nerve-racked men I had met a couple of weeks earlier. My appointment time was the one before his so he wished me good luck as my name was called. Sylvia did come along with me and Allison to this appointment and the senior nurse, Andrew, quickly confirmed the brilliant news that I was cancer-free. He said in all probability it was a case of prostatitis, but they needed to do a biopsy just to rule out some things. I left the hospital that day a very relieved man armed with a month's supply of antibiotics, to be followed by another blood test and a follow up appointment with the Consultant, Mr Phillips. As we were leaving the hospital later, we bumped into our Japanese friend, who had also received good news.

Aston Villa

On a more pleasurable note, or at least it is supposed to be, football of course is one of my great loves in life and following Aston Villa in particular. Recent years have been tough ones for my beloved famous club and it has not been easy being a devoted supporter. A bit like marriage though, you stick with it through thick and thin in the belief that you will come through stronger on the other side.

In my many years of supporting my favourite team, I had never once campaigned for the manager to be sacked. On this occasion, however, even I had to admit that the three years under the stewardship of Paul Lambert had gone past being a joke. Not only was the style of football very boring to watch (apart from one or two exceptions along the way), but we had broken so many unwanted records such as the club's biggest away defeat when we lost 8-0 to Chelsea, the largest number of home defeats in a season in the club's history and the lowest number of goals scored by any team, not only in the UK but indeed throughout Western Europe.

Those are just a few I can think of, but there are more unwanted records. The fact is that Aston Villa was sinking fast into relegation.

Something had to be done and I wrote a few emails to the recently appointed Chief Executive, Tom Fox. I stressed my love and passion for this great football club. I explained how I had been a committed supporter ever since the 1950's when my Dad took me to the games as a child. Tom, to be fair, replied to every email I sent him and I think he valued the fact that I was not seeking to be cruel towards anyone, but just wanted the very best for the club I have loved and supported for well over half a century.

Thankfully, after a humiliating defeat away to fellow relegation rivals Hull City, the club (or was it Tom Fox?) decided to pull the plug on Paul Lambert's reign as Aston Villa manager. A few days later, the inexperienced, but highly thought of Tim Sherwood was appointed and tasked with the responsibility of lifting the gloom following seven successive defeats and keeping Villa in the Premier League. In Sherwood's short time as temporary manager of Tottenham Hotspur he had developed a reputation as an outspoken manager with an eye for attacking football and encouraging younger players. He had a win ratio of around 50 per cent and now, having been in charge of Aston Villa for six games, he has the same ratio.

As football fans, Villa supporters have discovered what it is like to win games of football again and Sherwood has brought excitement back to the supporters with victories over our local rivals West Bromwich Albion in a spine-tingling FA Cup 6th round encounter to win us a place in the semi-final at Wembley. In the semi-final we were drawn to play the highly fancied Liverpool team. Aston Villa, however, on the day turned in an incredible performance, which shocked not only their own supporters, but indeed the whole football world as we ran out worthy winners by two goals to one. Ultimately in May we then played Arsenal in our first FA Cup Final since 2000, when we lost to Chelsea 1-0. Unfortunately we lost again this time too. Though Arsenal were brilliant on the day, running out as 4-0 victors, it is sad to say the Villa lads never really turned up to do themselves credit. The future does look brighter though with our effervescent young manager and his crop of new players.

It was a joy for Ian and myself to be present at both games. At the Cup Final I even had the chance of meeting my all-time Aston Villa hero Peter McParland. It was Peter who scored the two goals when Villa last won the FA Cup back in 1957 and I watched the match as a 9 year old on my Mum & Dad's nine inch black and white television. Peter and I met up at Starbucks for a coffee, chat and photographs before the game and that was a real thrill for me.

On the back of this, I feel I must stress how important I feel it is for parents to have special times with their children. Quality time set aside for fathers and sons and mothers and daughters are especially productive, not to mention necessary, in terms of bonding and creating those very special memories. I have said elsewhere that among my greatest memories of my own Dad, are the times we spent together at 'the Villa'. He took me to the games when I was a small lad and that established a friendship between us that lasted until the day he died aged 86. As I write about it now I am convinced I can still taste the Bovril and delicious pork pies we used to have in those days.

Now that Dad has been gone for nearly 10 years those special memories created while travelling to and from the football matches, as well as the time we were there stood together on the terraces, are more vivid and more valuable to me than ever before.

It does not have to be football of course, you can set up your own special moments set aside to be with your parents or children anytime and anywhere. It is the specific act of cultivating an interest together and prioritising that time together that creates that bond of love and appreciation that will last way beyond the grave. In the words of that great song by *Mike and the Mechanics*, do it now in the living years, while there is still time.

Raising Disability Awareness

HMRC did have one final event lined up for me to attend. I mentioned earlier that I had been chosen as one of the role models for a *Raising Disability Awareness* project that was being rolled out to all managers across HMRC. Well one year on and the project had not only been completed, but had been heralded as an unbridled success. Over 4,000 managers across the UK had attended the workshops and in excess of 50,000 members of staff impacted in some way by its message. The closing celebratory event was held at the Park Inn Hotel in Manchester and those present heard a number of inspiring speeches from people with disabilities who had been empowered to take on new challenges, and develop their careers as a result of the powerful message that was conveyed during the workshop sessions. Managers testified that they had grown in confidence when it came to working with people on their teams who had disabilities.

I attended this event with my daughter Sara, as Sylvia was not well enough to be there with me, and it was a joy to meet so many people from across HMRC of all grades. The *Raising Disability Awareness* project was supported 100 per cent by senior leaders from the main board in London and was a personal triumph for Derek Hughes, the Assistant Director of the business stream where

I had worked for the last few years, because this project had been his brainchild. You may recall I wrote earlier that Derek has a sister named Carole, who suffers from spina bifida, well, she was there as Derek's special guest, along with Robert, the man who has brought such joy into her life. Derek told the audience very movingly, of how Carole had been his inspiration and the reason why he is so passionate about championing the cause of people with disabilities. It was an amazing evening and one which made me feel really proud to have not only been part of the project, but to have belonged for so long to an organisation that has done so much to further the employment opportunities of people with disabilities. I for one, now leave the Civil Service with many wonderful memories and in HMRC I recognise a new type of leader is emerging that I am confident bodes well for the future of its workforce.

The end of a book and the start of a new chapter

Now it's 1st April 2015, and I am retired, but for what? There is no doubt in my mind that I have made the right choice. Certainly some six months ago it was not at all in my mind to retire this year, why should it have been when I was having such a ball at work? I was enjoying my regular day to day job working tax cases, I helped lead a thriving office-based Christian Fellowship group and I was receiving a number of invitations to go and speak at seminars, conferences and team meetings across HMRC. I was enjoying it all and it was providing Sylvia and me with a decent standard of living with my salary being boosted by my State Pension. Had HMRC not come up with this Voluntary Exit Scheme then I would have carried on until who knows when?

All things considered though this offer served to focus my mind and I now know this is the right time to re-fire into something new. First and foremost on my list of priorities though is to spend top quality time with my darling wife of 46 years. She has devoted herself to loving and caring for me and our children all these years and now it is her turn to receive something back. It is now over a year since Sylvia was flown home from Greece, and I know that she loves nothing more than lying in bed and holding my hand, just knowing I am there for her. There were times last summer, during those long nights of gorgeous sunshine, when my attitude was not the best to say the least. It was then I felt God spoke into my heart and said that my wife could be dead and I could then have had all the summer sunshine I ever wanted, but the fact is that she is alive and all she wants is you, so is that too much to ask? In all of the other things I might do from here on in, I must keep at the forefront of my mind that Sylvia is the love of my life and as such has first place. Now the Beatles song *I Want To Hold Your Hand* has taken on a whole new meaning for me.

That said, I am not the kind of person who can sit around and idle away my time. For instance, I cannot shake off those words I heard a few years back from Dr Chan Abraham. They live within me now as powerfully as the day I first heard them and they are motivating me to make a difference. If it is true (and my experiences of working with people suggest that it is) that the great majority of people in the UK are living a Monday to Friday death, because they dislike work and only live for the weekends, then that is desperately sad.

I remain convinced that life is an incredible gift and that each day we have breath is one to be celebrated. I come from the standpoint that we have each been created by God, each of us is totally unique and that every individual is not only wonderfully gifted, but also has a special reason to be here on planet earth, with a unique destiny to fulfil.

I have discovered that life is about choices. From the moment I first open my eyes in the morning, I can decide to smile and be full of gratitude for the gift of another day. I can decide that today I am going to do what I can to make the world I live in a better place by being kind, gentle, loving, compassionate, and generous with my words and forgiving in my attitudes. This kind of attitude does take a lot of practice, because it goes against the grain, particularly in the UK. As I alluded to earlier in this book, however, we can make the necessary changes to our personality by determining in our hearts. It is no excuse to say 'I am not that kind of person', or 'I am a pessimist by nature'. The fact is, we can change. I am a living example of that. All that most of us need is encouragement – there you are, that word has cropped up once again!

Because of the encouragement I have received and the mass of positive feedback I have had from my workplace presentations, I am convinced I can make a difference, not only in one person's life, but indeed to a whole team, or even a business. This stuff we call encouragement is more powerful than dynamite. It has the power to transform losers into winners, fear into faith, sorrow into joy and aimlessness into purpose.

During the course of my life I have had a number of people who have believed in me. At school I will never forget Mr Biddle, an English teacher, who first chose me to play in the school football team at the age of 12. From that moment on until I left school at the age of 15, Mr Biddle never left me out of the team. Instantly he became my favourite teacher and I began to work hard at English. No coincidence, therefore, it became the subject I was best at. Mr Biddle believed in me, as a result I became motivated and empowered.

Sylvia was my first ever serious girlfriend and I began to go out with her because she wrote to me and asked if we could meet up. Later when I asked her to marry me she gave me an immediate "Yes of course I will". Sylvia chose me. In doing that she demonstrated that she loved me and believed in me, and that empowered me to be her husband, to love her wholeheartedly and be loyal to her always.

My senior manager John Dolan, took the time to ring me and glowingly affirm the piece of work I had done. He went on to speak encouraging words about my communication skills and then he urged me on to a personal development programme. You see the pattern that has emerged. John's encouragement and belief in me, motivated me out of my very deep comfort zone and narrowness of thinking and empowered me to launch out as a public speaker and a writer. The gifts and talents were there all the time, but they just needed to be encouraged out.

I am convinced there are many thousands of people, young and old, who need to hear this message. I have a passion to get out there into the big wide world and deliver words of encouragement so that people, like me, will be motivated and empowered to enjoy life and begin to realise their potential. I am just beginning to do that at the age of 68, so why not you?

I have now launched my business as a motivational speaker, *John Flanner Motivates – Believes – Empowers*, and am working on the publication of my second book. If you are reading this right now, you will know I have been successful in the latter!

***

Appendix

Dame Cicely Saunders - her life and work

Born 22nd June 1918 in Barnet, Hertfordshire, Dame Cicely trained as a nurse, a medical social worker and finally as a physician. Involved with the care of patients with terminal illness since 1948, she lectured widely on this subject, wrote many articles and contributed to numerous books.

Dame Cicely founded St Christopher's Hospice in 1967 as the first hospice linking expert pain and symptom control, compassionate care, teaching and clinical research. St Christopher's has been a pioneer in the field of palliative medicine, which is now established worldwide. Through her single-minded vision, and the clinical practice and dissemination of her work through St Christopher's teaching and outreach, Dame Cicely revolutionised the way in which society cares for the ill, the dying and the bereaved. Her vision to establish her own home for the dying was underpinned by her religious faith. She had initially thought of creating an Anglican religious community but broadened her vision so that St Christopher's became a place that welcomed staff and patients of any faith or none. However, Cicely's strong Christian faith was a fundamental factor in her commitment to the dying and remained an anchor throughout her life.

Dame Cicely is recognised as the founder of the modern hospice movement and received many honours and awards for her work. She held more than 25 honorary degrees from the UK and overseas and awards included the British Medical Association Gold Medal for services to medicine, the Templeton Prize for Progress in Religion, the Onassis Prize for Services to Humanity, The Raoul Wallenberg Humanitarian Award and the Franklin D. Roosevelt Four Freedoms for Worship Medal.

Dame Cicely was made a Dame of the British Empire in 1979 and awarded the Order of Merit in 1989.

Dame Cicely Saunders recognised the inadequacy of the care of the dying that was offered in hospitals. So often, patients and families were told that "there was nothing more that could be done" a statement that Dame Cicely refused to accept. Throughout her time at St Christopher's her watchword was "there is so much more to be done."

Pioneering research on the use of morphine as an effective drug for pain control was carried out at St Christopher's, along with other detailed studies of new approaches to symptom control. Dame Cicely also understood that a dying person is more than a patient with symptoms to be controlled. She became convinced of the paramount importance of combining excellent medical and nursing care with 'holistic' support that recognised practical, emotional, social, and spiritual need. She saw the dying person and the family as the unit of care and developed bereavement services at St Christopher's Hospice to extend support beyond the death of the patient.

In 1969 Dame Cicely pioneered the first home care team taking St Christopher's care and philosophy out into the community. In 2001 St Christopher's Hospice received the Conrad N Hilton Humanitarian Prize - the world's largest humanitarian award - of one million dollars for the work originated by Dame Cicely through the Hospice. Dame Cicely Saunders died peacefully on Thursday 14th July 2005 at St Christopher's Hospice in south London, the world-famous hospice that she founded in the 1960s, and the birthplace of the modern hospice movement.

A Service of Thanksgiving for the life of Dame Cicely Saunders was held at Westminster Abbey on 8th March 2006.

Barbara Monroe, Chief Executive of St Christopher's Hospice, said,

> *"Dame Cicely's vision and work has transformed the care of the dying and the practice of medicine in the UK and throughout the world. She is an inspiration to us all.*
>
> *We had been caring for Dame Cicely at St Christopher's Hospice as a patient for some time. We will miss her very much. Her influence will carry on around the world as we work together in hospice and palliative care to support dying people and close to them.*
>
> *It is a privilege to share in Dame Cicely's vision and her work here at St Christopher's. We are dedicated to improving care for dying people everywhere."*

Allianz Global Press Release

1 IN 3 HOLIDAY MAKERS COULD BE TURNED AWAY FROM EUROPEAN HOSPITALS

Because they don't carry a European Health Insurance Card (EHIC)

"Don't Get Caught Out" Warns Allianz Global Assistance

A recent survey by Allianz Global Assistance reveals that 1 in 3 UK holidaymakers, don't travel with a European Health Insurance Card (EHIC), which entitles them to reduced or free medical care in the European Economic Area (EEC). Travelling without an EHIC could see UK holidaymakers stuck with hefty medical costs, or worse denied treatment, if they fall ill or have an accident.

John and Sylvia Flanner from Solihull, West Midlands found this out the hard way when they took a holiday to Greece without an EHIC. They didn't expect their trip to Zante to end in a trip to the hospital. Luckily, Allianz Global Assistance UK stepped in to assist the family through the emergency, underlining the value of adequate travel insurance cover, as well as the EHIC.

John, aged 66, has been blind since the age of 19. He was awarded an MBE in this year's Queen's Birthday Honour awards for services to Diversity and Equality, for his motivational speeches on living with a disability. However, when Sylvia, aged 64, suddenly developed a virus on holiday, which culminated in her having a stroke and being rushed to the local hospital, he was presented with a completely new challenge; the Flanners were travelling without an EHIC, and the hospital's medical team was reluctant to provide treatment.

The EHIC is available to all UK residents and allows travellers to receive treatment from public hospitals with the EEC and Switzerland. The EHIC allows travellers to get treatment on the same basis (for example, free or at a reduced cost) as people who live in that country. Holidaymakers need both their EHIC and travel insurance, as EHIC does not cover all medical costs, dental treatment or the cost of repatriation.

John's blindness, coupled with the language barrier, made it very difficult for him to communicate with the medical team, adding to an already highly stressful situation. The Flanner's son, Ian had no choice but to urgently fly to Zante. He also contacted his father's insurance company, Allianz Global Assistance UK, which took immediate pressure off the family, by sorting out the EHIC for Ian's parents. The Allianz Global Assistance UK team remained on hand throughout the coming days to assist the Flanner family, providing peace of mind at every step of the ordeal.

Greek hospitals don't provide ward nurses, making the family responsible for day-to-day care of the patient, such as changing drips and administering medicines; a call button for assistance from doctors is provided should the family need support. Rather than put more pressure on his blind father, Ian contacted the British Consulate and private 24/7 nursing cover for Sylvia was quickly arranged. However, it was soon clear that staying in a hospital in Greece, was not the best solution for Sylvia and Allianz Global Assistance arranged a private jet repatriation, flying Sylvia and John to Birmingham Airport and taking her to her hometown hospital.

Ian says, "I've done lots of travelling, but I've never heard of the EHIC. Allianz Global Assistance provided a first class service from start to finish; arranging the EHICs for my parents, as well as a doctor, who travelled with my mother from Birmingham airport, to the hospital in Solihull. This incident has really highlighted the importance of buying good travel insurance before you travel. I dread to think what could have happened, if Allianz Global Assistance hadn't been on hand to help us through this situation. We will make sure we all carry our EHIC with us for trips to Europe, as well as buying insurance – just in case."

Lee Taylor, Chief Sales Officer for Allianz Global Assistance UK comments, "The Flanner family were fortunate that Allianz Global Assistance was able to help them, but even with travel insurance, they couldn't get the medical attention they needed without an EHIC. This story underlines just how important it is to travel with an EHIC and adequate cover, yet our survey shows that 1 in 3 UK travellers don't take an EHIC with them to Europe. This puts them at huge risk, if they need medical care abroad. An EHIC card is essential for anyone to receive treatment from public hospitals in all European Economic Area countries

"We also urge holidaymakers to ensure they book the right level of travel insurance, declaring all medical conditions, as falling ill or needing emergency support abroad can be very costly. Travellers need to be aware of the risks they face, whether that's delayed or cancelled flights, lost luggage or something more serious such as an accident or illness. Only by having adequate travel insurance cover provides financial support, as well as expert advice when you need it most, as the Flanner family discovered."

July 2014

Acknowledgements

I wish to express my thanks to the following:

Staff at Bitzaro Palace for the level of compassion and kindness they showed to us as a family.

Staff at Buckingham Palace for their professional, courteous and welcoming manner.

Managers and colleagues at HMRC for allowing me to travel the country making Diversity and Inspirational presentations, when I could have been at my desk working on the job I was being paid to do.

Elizabeth Webb for her ceaseless encouragement - it was Liz, who first taught me that the "e" in email actually stands for "encouragement".

Kyle Cottington for kindly gifting me his website design – see www.edit.com

Clare Bugg for brilliantly writing my website pages and getting me on to Facebook and Twitter. (I just have to learn how to be proficient with them now!)

Dave Edwards for the superb business logo design, book cover design, artwork and photography. – www.studiodcreative.com

Rachel Edwards for faithfully proofreading and editing my two books – www.racheledwardswrites.com

My late Mum and Dad for making me (with God's help of course!) They would have been so proud to have been at Buckingham Palace.

My brother Paul and sisters Joan and Susan for their love, who themselves have had to cope with sight loss and ill health.

Our amazing children Beverley, Sara, Allison and Ian, who are proving to be such a source of strength at a time when Sylvia's health is so uncertain.

Sylvia for being a truly wonderful wife, mother and grandmother as well as being a fabulous friend to so many people. Thank you darling for (in the words of my favourite band The Bee Gees) staying alive.

A special dedication….

To the late great John Dolan, without whose intervention in my life, none of this would ever have happened. What John did for me will live in my memory forever. We did not know each other and in our work we were many grades apart. He did not have to do what he did, but he did it anyway. He picked up a telephone, said "Thank you, you have done a great job. Well done and by the way, did anyone ever tell you that you have great communication skills?"

That single act did not need a degree and it was not rocket science. It is something we can all do, i.e. encourage and affirm someone.

John was also a visionary leader because he looked into the future, saw how things were changing and was able to match my skill with those changes; all I needed was a little personal development and a bit of self-confidence. John invested in me and was not put off by my age, disability or that I was in a deep rut, a very nice little comfort zone indeed.

As a result of John's action and my cooperation literally thousands of people have been inspired and motivated by my story with still much more to come. As for me, I have achieved far more than I could ever have imagined and in writing my first book   "Fear, Fun and Faith" I fulfilled a desire that had been inside me for nearly 50 years.

It seems so unfair that John, who worked so hard on my nomination for the MBE never lived to see it. He tragically died just a few days into his retirement, ironically at a similar age to what I was when his words kick-started my life.

I say it again, encouragement is dynamite and no-one ever died from an overdose of the stuff, so come on, let us dish it out in great measure, you just never know what talent you may be releasing for the benefit of mankind.

May these words, offered in humility, bring some comfort to John's widow, Jane, to his two children, family and friends.

The final word

Thanks to God my Father, Jesus Christ my Saviour and to the Holy Spirit, my comforter, counsellor and friend through whom I have received the precious gift of everlasting life.

John Flanner MBE

www.johnflanner.co.uk

Email: john@flanner.co.uk

Fear Fun and Faith

John Flanner was a typical football mad teenager until he was robbed of his sight at the age of 19 to a rare hereditary condition. As a shy, self-deprecating young man growing up in 1960's Birmingham, John was already battling many fears and phobias before his subsequent blindness plunged him into a world of darkness.

However, John's determination to succeed, faith in God and the ability to see the potential in every situation led to the rise of a Brummie born man who conquered his fears and the business world with it. John was the first recipient of the prestigious National Civil Service Diversity Award in 2006 and is now a sought after motivational speaker using his personal experiences in overcoming unexpected disability to inspire and encourage businessmen and women across the UK.

Fear Fun and Faith is the inspirational story of an ordinary man who has led an extraordinary life. Join John as he takes you through the twists and turns of his personal journey with his trademark humour and witty writing style, peppered with plenty of emotional anecdotes and more than one miracle along the way.

Fear Fun and Faith is available in all good book stores

ISBN 978-0-9934175-0-4